Church of All Worlds
Clergy Handbook

Compiled by Oberon Zell, Primate (Editor)
and the CAW Clergy Pathways Committee (CPC)

CAW Precepts

(from the CAW Membership Handbook, *3rd Edition, 1997)*

1. Be Excellent to Each Other!
2. Be Excellent to Yourself!
3. Honor Diversity!
4. Take Personal Responsibility!
5. Consider the Consequences!
6. Walk Your Talk!

Church of All Worlds
Post Office Box 1359
Nebo, NC 28761 USA
www.CAW.org

Zell, Oberon, 1942-

92 pp.

ISBN: 979-8-3304-4634-6

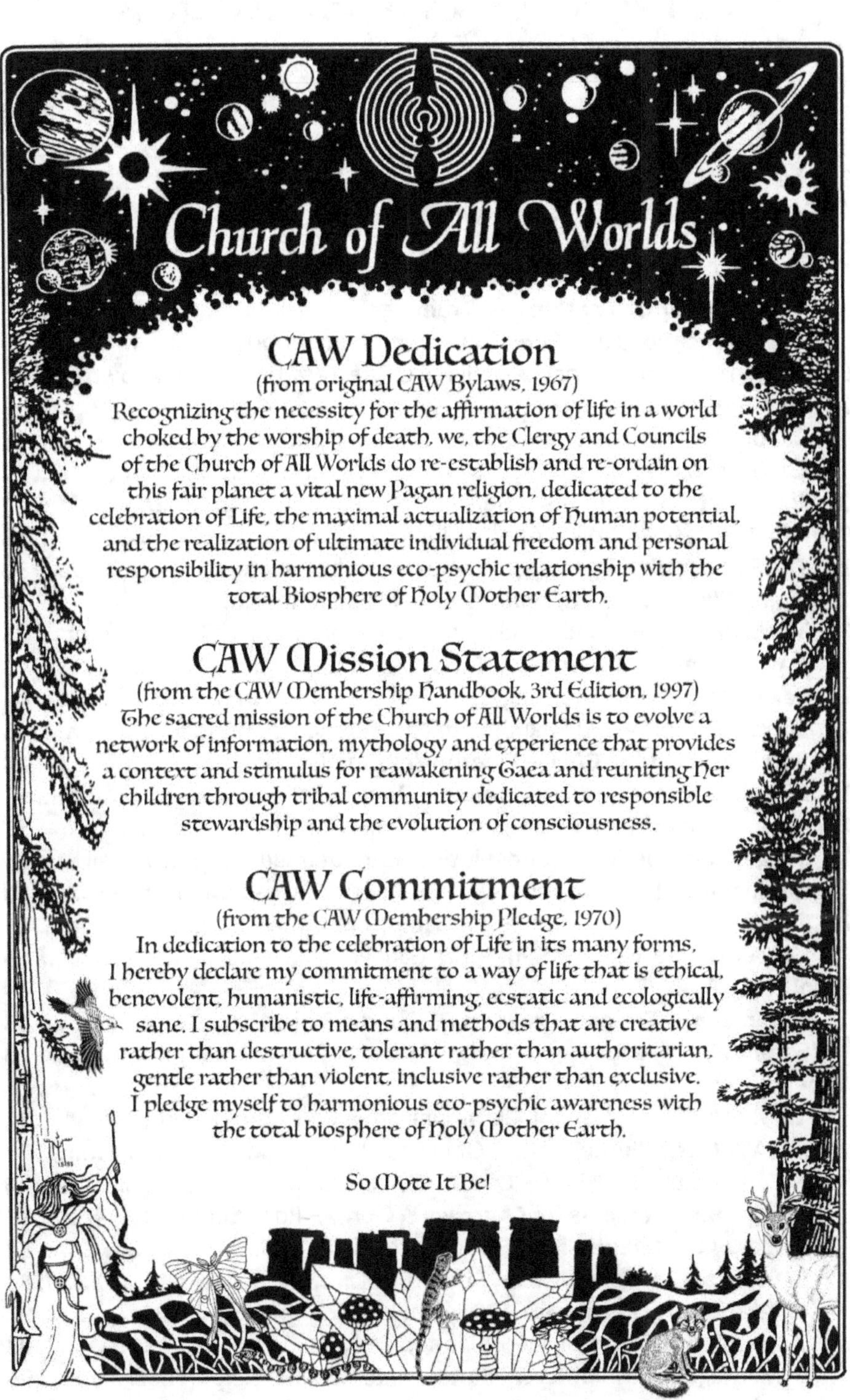

Church of All Worlds

CAW Dedication
(from original CAW Bylaws, 1967)
Recognizing the necessity for the affirmation of life in a world
choked by the worship of death, we, the Clergy and Councils
of the Church of All Worlds do re-establish and re-ordain on
this fair planet a vital new Pagan religion, dedicated to the
celebration of Life, the maximal actualization of Human potential,
and the realization of ultimate individual freedom and personal
responsibility in harmonious eco-psychic relationship with the
total Biosphere of Holy Mother Earth.

CAW Mission Statement
(from the CAW Membership Handbook, 3rd Edition, 1997)
The sacred mission of the Church of All Worlds is to evolve a
network of information, mythology and experience that provides
a context and stimulus for reawakening Gaea and reuniting Her
children through tribal community dedicated to responsible
stewardship and the evolution of consciousness.

CAW Commitment
(from the CAW Membership Pledge, 1970)
In dedication to the celebration of Life in its many forms,
I hereby declare my commitment to a way of life that is ethical,
benevolent, humanistic, life-affirming, ecstatic and ecologically
sane. I subscribe to means and methods that are creative
rather than destructive, tolerant rather than authoritarian,
gentle rather than violent, inclusive rather than exclusive.
I pledge myself to harmonious eco-psychic awareness with
the total biosphere of Holy Mother Earth.

So Mote It Be!

CAW Clergy Handbook
Contents

1. CAW Clergy Defined

By Oberon Zell, Primate

CLERGY ARE DEFINED LEGALLY AS: "INDIVIDUALS WHO ARE DULY ordained, commissioned or licensed by a religious body constituting a church or church denomination. They are given the authority to conduct religious worship, perform sacerdotal functions and administer ordinances or sacraments according to the prescribed tenets and practices of that church or denomination." *(U.S. Social Security Self Employment publication #533)*

The Church of All Worlds offers both **Ministerial Licensing** and **Priesthood Ordination**, which are separate processes. The term "minister" is derived from the Latin word *minister* (gen. *ministri*), which means a servant to a higher good, recognized through a process of formal investiture. In CAW, ministers are licensed through an application process, indicating prior experience and training, reasons for wanting to be licensed, and letters of recommendation. Ministers are licensed to perform legal sacraments, marriages, rites of passage, prison and hospital visitations, chaplaincies, etc. These need not be specifically CAW-Trad, but may be as generic as appropriate.

CAW Priests and Priestesses require considerably more training and experience than Ministers in CAW's particular history, practice, liturgy, theology and philosophy. In addition to the Ministerial functions described above, our ordained Priests and Priestesses also need to be adept in pastoral counseling, divination, ritual creation, administration, teaching, group dynamics, and public speaking. They must have theological understanding as well as liturgical skills. As CAW is a Bardic tradition, having theatrical experience and a repertoire of chants and songs is a particularly relevant qualification. Just like 19th-century Christian missionaries, a CAW Priest or Priestess is expected to be able to go to any remote place and establish a functional extension of the CAW; as well as be an effective representative of CAW at interfaith conferences, Pagan gatherings, etc. And finally, they need to have the support of a congregation who value their service and acknowledge them as Clergy.

Obviously, in order to be either licensed or ordained as Clergy in the Church of All Worlds, one must be a currently active member. Join and apply at www.CAW.org.

NOTE: In view of the epidemic of sexual and other forms of abuse currently surfacing in certain other religious organizations, the protection of innocents is a primary concern of the Church of All Worlds. Therefore we require prospective Clergy to sign a sworn statement that they have never perpetrated criminal abuse or victimization of others. We will not license or ordain any persons who have been so convicted in the past, nor any persons who for reasons of neglect or abuse have been compelled by the state to surrender the custody of minor children; and it is our policy to immediately suspend Clergy standing upon any such charges being filed, and revoke Clergy standing upon conviction for any crimes involving abuse of children or others. We offer compassion, counseling and support for abuse victims and their families.

2. The Work of a CAW Priest or Priestess

by Anodea Judith, High Priestess

An active Priest or Priestess of the Church of All Worlds is expected to...

A. BE AN ACTIVE RELIGIOUS AND SPIRITUAL LEADER FOR A CAW CONGREGATION, WHICH MAY INCLUDE:

1. Mentoring Nests and other CAW members;
2. Understanding and practicing Clergy Confidentiality;
3. Training apprentices to become future Clergy of CAW;
4. Designing/scripting/leading CAW rituals large and small;
5. Channeling and aspecting Divinity in rituals and Mysteries;
6. Facilitating and being an active member of a Nest or Branch;
7. Teaching classes and/or workshops for CAW members and others;
8. Planning/facilitating/sponsoring CAW festivals or other major events;
9. Mediating disputes according to the "CAW Guidelines for Conflict Resolution;"
10. Providing wise Pastoral Counseling (sex, relationships, abuse, grief, divination, etc.);
11. Performing rites of passage, initiations, and other personal rituals for CAW members and others.

B. BE AN ACTIVE, PARTICIPATING MEMBER OF THE CLERGY COUNCIL, WHICH MAY INCLUDE:

1. Participating in Clergy visioning;
2. Contributing to CAW Handbooks, etc.
3. Participating in on-line communications;
4. Attending regional and national meetings;
6. Maintaining contact with fellow Clergy members;
6. Helping to draft official position statements based on CAW precepts.

C. BE A LEADER IN THE NATIONAL CAW ORGANIZATION; DISSEMINATE THE CAW VISION TO ALL. THIS MAY INCLUDE:

1. Writing for CAW blogs & publications;
2. Serving on an active CAW Council or Committee;
3. Participating on one or more e-lists and/or FaceBook;
4. Giving interviews on CAW and Paganism to various media;
5. Representing CAW as an ambassador at interfaith conferences;
6. Serving on the Board of Directors or National Management Council;
7. Understanding and articulating CAW philosophy, theology, precepts and Vision to others.

3. The Priesthood: Parameters and Responsibilities

By Nema

(Excerpt from *The Priesthood: Parameters and Responsibilities,* 1995)

"The Priesthood is a condition of a soul on fire with love. The Priesthood is a way of life demanded by a certain level of spiritual responsibility, a way of life that focuses action and non-action toward universal enlightenment."

THE PRIEST IS NOT A MESSIAH OR SAVIOR; HIS OR HER FUNCTION IS not one of redemption or salvation, but of realization and evolution. A priest is a human among humans, motivated by enlightened self-interest. The sooner universal enlightenment is complete, the sooner the Priest will be free of the obligation of individual continuity and can resolve into pure undifferentiated Intelligence.

A second function of Priesthood is that of information sharing. As mentioned earlier, the elder Brothers and Sisters share wisdom with the younger, the younger Brothers and Sisters share new points-of-view. At our present stage of evolution, the Priest shares Information in ways suitable to his partners in dialogue.

Through his/her own experiments and experiences in self-knowledge, the Priest becomes ever more accurate at assessing the spiritual level of development of another person. From this assessment the Priest fashions and uses the most appropriate persona or Mask, through which he/she communicates with the other person. The Priest seems familiar, compatible, comfortable; the other person relaxes and opens in receptivity.

Information-sharing can also occur through the practice of Art. One virtue of Art as a tool in the Great Work is its ability to move and change the audience through bypassing the verbal censors of the unbalanced Ego. Art evokes response from the beholder. A good artist knows precisely which responses he/she wants to evoke, in what order and/or combination; he/she also has the skill to present the proper stimuli to accomplish it. Each medium of Art has its particular strengths and weaknesses.

Music can evoke emotional and spiritual responses. It Communicates directly with our chakras; the precision and power of music's Influence depends directly on the composer's and performer's genius. In the most sublime music, such as that of Bach and Beethoven, the evocation is of Intelligence itself and the ecstasy of the rapt listener.

Dance and mime evoke sympathy and relational openness from the audience. It also evokes admiration and awe of the human form in motion. As a species, we take pleasure in beauty, skill, grace, power and heart, all essential ingredients for the action-arts. Graphic art, architecture and sculpture can evoke the entire spectrum of human response. The same holds true for still photography and motion pictures.

No matter what the medium, a talented Priest can communicate the great fact of our unity without preaching or didacticism. Art shows rather than tells. All great artists function as Priests, whether they think of themselves as Priests or not.

In addition to the talismanic and information-sharing functions, the Priest performs Temple-work as a ritualist in order to Augment sensitivity to the flow of the Magickal Current, to formally align his/her being with the Current, to add all the power. and energy he/she is capable of channeling to the Current.

The Priest and the rest of the race participate in the actual generation of the Magickal Current. The collective electromagnetic energy of the human nervous system imparts a particular signature-signal on the carrier wave of the flow of time and universal energy. The force of our human signal returns amplified by its circuit of intergalactic space. Upon returning to Earth, the signal is received by all those with any degree of psychic sensitivity. The evolved signal is very attractive to those with clear vision. The sensitives begin to put the signal into practice, and the next pulse of the human signal Is much stronger going in. Our physical/technological history grows exponentially, and so does the force of the evolved signal.

The ritualistic function of the Priesthood is as important as the other functions. A Priest's ritual technique differs from that of the Adept in that it is minimalist and often done in motionless silence.

A Priest gives advice when sincerely asked to do so and has the right to intervene and comment whenever he/she sees fit. A Priest doesn't debate, argue, convince, or prove. A Priest speaks Truth in the most appropriate way possible but doesn't try to sell his/her statements to anyone. Accepting or rejecting Truth when it's presented is the responsibility of the listener.

The Priest functions as spiritual counselor, healer of souls, speaker of truth. He/she is an explorer who returns to tell of high adventure and wondrous visions, then works to help all interested listeners to befit themselves for the journey. The Priest has experienced humanity's next step in evolution and from this experience works wholeheartedly for the rest of the race to take the step also.

The Priest functions as a warrior who battles restrictive dogmas in all their many guises. When appropriate, the Priest participates In and encourages the Outer political processes, doing whatever is possible to restructure the forms of society to, better reflect the unity of Intelligence in the legislative process.

When our transformation is complete as a species. There will be no need for legislation, the state, national boundaries or artificial control of the flow of goods and services. There will be no need for armies, police, or prisons. The concept of wealth will be redefined; churches. corporations, charities and clubs based on exclusivity will be greatly changed or will disappear entirely. In the meantime, the Priest exercises wisdom and creativity in using existing channels to assist the great leap humanity is facing.

Parameters of Priesthood vary with the situation and the Individuals involved in it. To better enable oneself to work efficiently at all times the Priest practices and continues to grow in knowledge, understanding, wisdom and silence. Any situation is best handled from the plane(s) above the plane in which it is occurring. This provides an overview from which to see the situation in context, thus permitting the optimum resolution to be perceived.

By operating from the vantage of the Supernals (the Spheres of understanding, wisdom and silence), the Priest perceives and acts from the highest possible overview. Through habitual exercise, the Supernal view is maintained at all times--as an ideal situation. In practice, prevailing social attitudes insinuate themselves into any Individual's thought processes, almost by osmosis, due to the sheer numbers of uninitiates in the world and the strength of their combined psychic fields. In order to combat the situation, it's helpful to design one's personal environment to remind one of the Supernal view, to engage in daily practice that reinforces the view, to carry on one's person an amulet or talisman to remind one of the Priestly office.

There is no such thing as resting on one's laurels or retirement in the Priesthood. It's truly a life's work, and more. Death itself is merely a short vacation or sabbatical that permits one to obtain a fresh and energetic vehicle through which to operate. An individual who has developed enough to see and embrace the Priesthood has also developed the strength of personal integration sufficient to survive intact through any number of deaths and births. To those who see personal survival as the antithesis of our course of returning to the Nothingness from whence we came, It might be said that Personal dissolution cannot be complete until all are able to release their hold on illusion. The unity of Intelligence prevents selective dissolution.

The Priesthood's task is to make the unity of Intelligence obvious to the whole of the human racer, so that this unity can also prevent the nightmare of nuclear annihilation. We live in a crucial time; each Individual Is responsible for our continuity and development. The Priesthood is the cadre of those who have fully accepted this responsibility.

Every facet of life participates in the work of the Priest. No ordinary motivation could Inspire total dedication to such an enormous task.

Only the experience of the unity of Intelligence, the experience of participating in the universal pattern of Consciousness can enable one to actually love one's neighbor as oneself. Our neighbor is ourself in the unity of Intelligence, and much of ourself is in pain through Ignorance of this fact. There Is nothing that is not of us. All that is we embrace in joyful recognition of our essential unity and Identity.

The Priesthood is a condition of a soul on fire with love.

Church of All Worlds Founders Oberon Zell & Richard Lance Christie,
at Arches National Monument, Moab, Utah, 2005.

4. CAW Clergy in the 21ˢᵗ Century

By Oberon *(April 25, 2009;*
updated Dec. 23, 2011; Feb. 9, 2012; Dec. 24, 2014)

THE CHURCH OF ALL WORLDS ORIGINATED AT WESTMINSTER College in Fulton, MO, on April 7, 1962, when Lance Christie and I—having just read Heinlein's sci-fi novel, *Stranger in a Strange Land*—first shared water and pledged our lives to the actualization of the precepts and principles found in that book, and in Abraham Maslow's concepts of self-actualization. We soon added many others to our growing water-brotherhood, which we called "Atl" (the Aztec word for "water," with the esoteric meaning of "ancient home of our ancestors").

During the first five years, Atl was an underground secret society, but we debated continually over becoming public so we could reach other potential people like us. In 1967, we decided to have it both ways, and diverge into two branches—one private and one public. Lance was selected to head up the continuing private branch—initially the Atlan Foundation, which much later incorporated as the Association for the Tree of Life (ATL).

Now living in St Louis, I was chosen to lead the public branch as the Church of All Worlds, which presented itself to the world over Labor Day of 1967, defining ourselves for the first time as "Pagan." This began what we have come to call the 2ⁿᵈ Phase of CAW, during which we incorporated the Church (March 4, 1968), started our flagship magazine *Green Egg* (March 21, 1968), opened our first public Temples, developed our 9-circle program of self-actualization, and ordained our first Priests (myself and Don Wildgrube) and Priestesses (Carolyn Clark and Morning Glory). We thus became the first church in modern history to legally ordain women as Priestesses!

The 2ⁿᵈ Phase lasted until 1978, at which time, with many of the key personnel having moved to California, CAW Central in St Louis folded, and *Green Egg* ceased publication. For several years CAW languished in Limbo, functioning only through several subsidiaries in NorCalifia, such as Forever Forests, the Holy Order of Mother Earth (HOME), and the Ecosophical Research Association (ERA).

In 1985 we began the 3ʳᵈ Phase of CAW, holding Board Meetings, electing officers, and ordaining a whole new slate of Clergy, including the incomparable Anodea Judith (ordained at Beltaine of 1985), who served as both High Priestess and BoD President for seven years, during which time she became known as our "Presitess." *Green Egg* was revived in 1988, and CAW went on to again become a major force in the worldwide Pagan community. This phase lasted until 2002, when a hostile takeover by our Ohio-based Board of Directors led to a complete collapse and attempted dissolution of the Church.

The 4ᵗʰ and current Phase began at Beltane of 2005, and became known as "the 3ʳᵈ Phoenix Resurrection" of CAW.

In the Old Days of CAW (i.e. 1967-2002), progress through the RINGS led to automatic ordination into the Priesthood at 7ᵗʰ Circle. We aren't doing that in this current 3ʳᵈ Phase. While we still expect much of the criteria of attaining 7ᵗʰ Circle to apply to potential Priests and Priestesses, this is no longer a direct correlation. Some of this training may come from elsewhere—such as the programs of other Traditions and Schools. And that training will count for CAW as well.

And most important—attaining 7th Circle in CAW is now associated more with the original concept of self-actualization, and CAW members of the 3rd Ring (i.e. Circles 7-9) are now known as "Beacons" rather than "Clergy." They may or may not also be ordained, but that is no longer a given just because they've attained the 3rd Ring. Consider the role and title of "Beacons" to be non-clerical, reflecting rather that such folks have come a long way in their personal evolution towards self-actualization, and will hopefully be a shining example to others. Beacons are elders, mentors, exemplars, inspirational visionaries, leaders (as in "on the leading edge"), authorities (as in "authoritative," NOT "authoritarian"), sages, mages, etc.

But CAW Priests and Priestesses are those who have a specific calling towards religious service to the CAW community and beyond. They are be expected to have a firm grasp of CAW liturgy (as presented in our book, *Creating Circles & Ceremonies*), and be able to design and conduct rites and rituals as called upon: handfastings, baby blessings, rites of passage, initiations, funerals, Nest meetings, Sabbat rites, Mysteries, etc.

They must be able to provide pastoral counseling and have a firm grasp of clergy confidentiality. In essence, CAW Priests and Priestesses should be able (like 19-century Christian missionaries) to go to some far-off place and establish a full CAW religious presence and create a local CAW community in accord with the premises and principles of the CAW Tradition. Clergy applications ask for experience, credentials, references, essays on vocational calling and why one wants to serve in this capacity; as well as supportive petitioning and testimonials from the congregation that wants them to be so recognized.

Training for CAW Priests and Priestesses should reflect and be at least somewhat equivalent to the kind of training offered in seminaries for the Clergy of other faiths. We wish to utilize other available programs, such as those offered by Earth Traditions Ministry, Cherry Hill Seminary, Woolston-Steen Theological Seminary, Star King Divinity School, Grey School of Wizardry, etc. This will enable our Clergy and Clergy candidates to pick up additional training and experience they may not already have.

Separate from the issue of CAW Priesthood, however, we also offer simple Ministerial licensing. The criteria for this are far less extensive than those for CAW Priests and Priestesses, as Ministers are not be expected to provide a full range of Clergy services to the CAW community. A Ministerial License from CAW entitles the bearer to perform weddings (and sign the certificate), visit people in prisons or hospitals, serve as Chaplains in prisons and military, etc.—wherever a legal Ministerial License would be useful.

For Ministerial licensing, we have a simple application form and some appropriate interview questions. We encourage any who feel the call to Clergy service to first get a Ministerial License, and then, only if they feel a further call to religious service within the CAW community itself, should they pursue further training and ordination into the Priesthood. But if not, no further training would be required or expected of them.

All Clergy Applications are reviewed and approved by the CAW's Elder Priesthood. In addition, Clergy applicants in other countries than the USA which have their own National Management Council (NMC) must be acceptable to said NMC; we will not license or ordain any Clergy in other countries against the wishes of their own NMC.

Church of All Worlds

PO Box 1359, Nebo, NC 28761 USA
www.CAW.org

5. Pagan Clergy

By Oberon Zell, Primate, Church of All Worlds

Part I: Priests and Priestesses

(from *Green Egg*, Vol. 29, No. 113; May-June 1996)

T THE SECOND PANTHEACON FESTIVAL HELD IN FEBRUARY OF 1996 in San Jose, I attended a panel on "Pagan Clergy." This discussion evidenced a trend I have noticed over the years. Every attempt to talk about this subject seems to break down around definitions: What, exactly, does it mean to be a "Priest" or "Priestess"? Is it the same thing as being "Clergy"? And, of course, the issue always comes around eventually to that of *paid* Clergy, which seems to get everybody jumping up and down on their end of the "Group W bench." So naturally I have to put my two *sisterti* in…

I think the present confusion began when Gerald Gardner decided to proclaim Witchcraft to be "The Old Religion," referring to all his Witches as "Priests" and "Priestesses." Upon receiving the first degree, the new initiate is told, "Arise Witch and Priest (or Priestess)!" Many Wiccans today regard all members of the coven as fellow Priests and Priestesses, with the only distinction being made by regular folks and the "High" Priest/ess. This attitude carried over into such early groups as "The Pagan Way" (founded in 1969), which regarded Pagans as comprising the "outer court" of Witchcraft, as if everyone in the Pagan community was pursuing an initiatory path whose culmination was 3^{rdo} Witchcraft! I have even heard it said by some of the Craft that "Witches are the Clergy and Pagans are the laity" of our movement. And last year, at the first Pantheacon, Francesca Dubie (Faerie Trad), one of the most respected Witches of the West, throwing up her hands at the panel on Pagan Clergy, said, "Oh, what does it matter what we call ourselves? We're all Witches, aren't we?"

Well, no, Francesca, we're not. And this is the source of the problem. Some of us Pagans who are not Witches are Druids, Greeks, Egyptians, Norse, Celts…even

Hindus, Shinto, Native Americans, Africans or Polynesians. To say nothing of the Church of All Worlds, which defies categorization. In those Pagan traditions which are more tribal in their social structure, there may be no "Clergy" as such at all; there are instead village shamans, of which I believe traditional European Witches to have been the equivalent. Shamans (as Witches) are herbalists, magicians, psychopomps, doctors, counselors, midwives and psychic voyagers; but they are not usually Priest/esses. That is, they seldom actually conduct the rituals of the religious practice. The "Old Religion" was not Witchcraft; it was (and is) Paganism.

While Witchcraft in former times may not have been the actual religion of the people, it certainly was a craft, a practice, perhaps even an initiatory cult as it is described in Leland's *Aradia*. Modern Wicca, however, is becoming a full-blown religion in its own right, currently comprising nearly half the Pagan community. Nonetheless, the basic congregational structure in the Craft remains that of the coven, with generally no more than 3-13 members meeting once a month, usually in someone's living room or back yard, rather than in a "temple" consecrated only for that purpose (although even this is changing…). A single individual "HP" or "HPs" may perform all the rituals, or they may be conducted in turn by each of the coveners. Sometimes such a HP or HPs may also teach the Craft, or do readings, spells and special rituals; but these responsibilities are often incidental. In this model, by far the most common in the Craft, being a Priest or Priestess is certainly not a full-time profession.

It should thus be understood that there are several meanings to the terms "Priest" and "Priestess." As in the Craft, anyone who keeps an altar, who serves the Gods, may be so designated. So may the one who is conducting the ritual this evening. And these terms may also be used to denote those who serve the greater community in a temple, church, or other organizational structure. Don Frew, a dedicated Pagan representative on Bay Area interfaith councils, sitting on the Pantheacon II panel, offered an insightful distinction between "Priest/esses" and "Clergy" in which the former are more individual, while the latter are more institutional. This is like the distinction I make between "spirituality" and "religion." I agree with him and think much of the confusion may indeed be coming from an assumption that being a Priest/ess in a small coven is the equivalent of being a member of the Clergy in a large church.

Most contemporary religions require extensive training of their professional (i.e. paid) Clergy, including pastoral counseling, public speaking, theology, administration, etc. This training is accomplished through years of accredited seminary instruction and internship. Additionally, they must be called by a denomination to serve and be ordained; and they must then win the trust and confidence of a congregation that is willing to engage their services. Parts II and III of this series will focus on expectations and qualifications for ordination and service of Pagan Clergy.

Now there are some Wiccan groups, such as the Church of Iron Oak, the New Wiccan Church, or the Aquarian Tabernacle Church, that have gone far beyond the traditional coven model and have actually organized legal Wiccan "churches," with all that implies, including professional Clergy. And some of the afore-mentioned Pagan traditions also have trained and ordained Clergy. These are most commonly called "Priests" and "Priestesses." (Indeed, it should be noted here that only Pagan religions have "Priestesses.") Some aspire to a restoration of temples to the Gods, with elaborate rituals conducted for the whole community. Some of these are indeed engaged full-time in their priestly vocations, with no time left over for a mundane job. If the talents of such dedicated people are to continue to be made available to the community, and we are not to burn out our very best and most committed, they need to be supported by the communities they serve.

So then arises the question of "paid Clergy"—probably the most contentious issue in modern Paganism. In the Olden Days, of course, the Priesthood was a full-time occupation, and such individuals generally lived in the temples, monasteries or other sacred facilities, which provided for all their needs. These facilities were, in turn, supported by the towns or cities that they served. Indeed, writing seems actually to have been invented in the temples as a means of keeping records of inventories and donations. Even in tribal villages, when one required the services of the local Shaman or Witch, it was customary to bring them a chicken or other gift; or at least offer to haul water or chop firewood! Carlos Castaneda always brought a bag of groceries whenever he visited Don Juan. Contemporary church congregations are asked to contribute a *tithe* (10% of their incomes) to the support of their preachers. It is the height of rudeness to *expect* a professional to offer their services for free, whether they are a doctor, lawyer, prostitute or shaman.

The question is one of how much support a given congregation can muster—and this is between the professionals and their clients, or constituencies. There are other ethical considerations here as well: witness those who charge astronomical fees for their services, preying on people's vulnerabilities and needs for authentic growth and healing. I personally feel that a fair deal is time-for-time. That is, if someone wants an hour of my time for, say, counseling, I expect an hour of theirs in return. Whether this be in the cash form of an hour's worth of their wages, or an hour's worth of services such as cleaning my house or giving me a massage, I feel a fair exchange must be made. For those growing numbers of Pagan Clergy who are engaged full-time, and thus unavailable to hold down a "day job," if every member of their congregations tithed to their support, most might be able to get by.

There is a place and a need for many forms of leadership in our diverse community. We must find better ways of empowering, supporting and honoring our highly-skilled and committed leaders. And thus do we empower ourselves.

CAW Banner by Anodea Judith, 1990.

Part II: Mail-order Ordinations vs. Training

(from *Green Egg*, Vol. 29, No. 114; July-August 1996)

FEW MONTHS AGO *GREEN EGG* RECEIVED A COMMUNICATION which read: "Please inform your readers about the Universal Life Church, Inc. which exists to allow people of all religions the right to become ordained ministers & perpetuate religious freedom…their willingness to ordain anyone, irrespective of religion, for free could have an enormous impact on the Pagan community…it might bear having an article in GE about the opportunity for Pagans to become legally ordained [with] an established organization behind them."

The ULC no doubt seemed a very neat idea when Pentecostal Reverend Kirby J. Hensley founded it back in 1959, and Hensley is truly an inspired visionary (albeit also a nut-case), who occasionally makes a sort of weird sense (quote from him: "The three most important things in life are sex, food, and freedom; and anyone who doesn't try to get as much of all three as possible is a damn fool!"). He came up with this nifty notion that anyone oughtta be able to define his own personal spiritual trip as a legitimate religion, and if the government was gonna grant special privileges and exemptions to established churches, then anybody who wanted to should be able to get in on the deal. So he offered to ordain anyone who sent him five bucks. Cool, huh?

But here's the rub: being a Priest or Priestess is a *calling* requiring considerable skills, commitment, training and character. Not everyone is so called, and many who are may be unsuitable. The assumption here is that being Clergy is a simple task requiring no skills or training whatsoever (let alone character), and in Hensley's case (a self-ordained Fundamentalist Christian preacher), he's probably right.

But a Pagan Priest or Priestess needs to be a skilled ritualist, counselor, teacher, community organizer, magician, healer, loremaster/mistress, therapist, spiritual guide, theologian, historian, folklorist, visionary, etc. This Work calls for knowledge and expertise in herbalism, mythology, rites of passage, chants, music, drumming, shamanic journeying, spells, talismans, divination, personal counseling (sex, relationships, addictions, abuse, grief…), conflict mediation, psychotherapy, and possibly even midwifery. A Priest/ess must have a spiritual calling and a personal relationship with the Gods and be able to channel and carry the energies of a group ritual. They must be psychologically together, personally responsible, authoritative but non-authoritarian, compassionate, wise, and charismatic enough to hold a group together. Moreover, this is a lifetime commitment, not to be undertaken lightly.

Ordination is the culmination of extensive and highly specialized training designed to ensure that a person is fully qualified to undertake the incredible responsibility of the Work. Without the training, any "Certificate of Ordination" is utterly meaningless. Frankly, it annoys me no end that people would think that an "ordination" obtained from "Bishop" Hensley is equivalent to one achieved after years of training! By their practice of mail-order ordinations without any study or training, ULC has unwittingly created a system which has served to discredit the whole idea of ordination. This opinion is widely held, with the ULC generally regarded as a scam. Claiming ULC ordination would certainly not improve one's credibility with the authorities, let along the Pagan community!

To this my correspondent replied:

"...We all know it's not about a deep commitment to a particular religion. There is no training given (unless you want to study their mail courses), & I don't think they claim anything like an absolute & in-depth ordination program. But, you see, there is the point that it's *legal*. Through the ULC, my Priestess—an initiate of our tradition—was able to legally perform my handfasting when it became clear that the Covenant of the Goddess credentials weren't going to be here on time. It was important to me to have our religious ceremony legal—it pisses me off that it isn't automatically so.

"What I'm saying is that I've found the ULC to be useful to me. Pagans must press on for changes—we want to marry, name & bury our own with no interference from the authorities. But we are so scattered & diverse that it is almost impossible to get ourselves recognized--& there is an enormous fear of imposing dogma & doctrine on ourselves. We need something to back us up; if it's the ULC for the interim, so be it. It's surely one option. After all, it wouldn't be the first time that a shaky organization has been used to good ends. I'm simply pointing out how it can be used to our own ends, as a short term weapon against the persecution we face. There has to be something to bind us, of our many traditions & beliefs, together without killing growth & diversity."

Well sure, and maybe I'd like to be allowed to perform brain surgery, and maybe I could find some fly-by-night outfit that would, like the Wizard of Oz, give me a diploma certifying me to be a bona-fide brain surgeon. But unless I have the skills and training needed to actually *perform* brain surgery, this certificate isn't worth the fake parchment it's printed on, and I would be grossly irresponsible if I were to go around claiming, on the basis of having this diploma, that I *was* a brain surgeon. And imagine if I solicited people actually in need of such surgery to have me operate on them! We no more need a bunch of untrained people conducting sacred rites on the authority of a ULC certificate that we need unqualified quacks with a mail-order MD diploma attempting to practice medicine.

If you feel truly called to become a Pagan Priest or Priestess, please be responsible and become qualified for the job! Most Pagan and Wiccan groups have their own training programs—some relatively simple, and some highly complex, each according to the needs of that particular tradition. The Church of All Worlds, for instance, has a program of Clergy training that takes a minimum of three years, and you can bet that an ordained CAW Priest or Priestess is not only legal, but fully qualified!

If someone in the Pagan community wants to get legally married, there are an ever-growing number of legally-ordained Pagan Clergy around to do the job. Most Pagan groups labeled "churches," and many others as well, can provide such Clergy upon request, or a helpful referral. It simply isn't necessary, desirable, or ethical that every member of the congregation has to be Clergy!

And as for having "something to bind us, of our many traditions & beliefs, together without killing growth & diversity"...well, that's what our growing networks of alliances and federations are for. It's my fervent hope and millennial dream that such associations as the Covenant of the Goddess, Pagan Federation, Pan-Pacific Pagan Alliance, Association of Earth Religion Churches, Universal Federation of Pagans, Pagan Interfaith Assembly, Pagan Web and others will ultimately coalesce into a seamless vast interconnected system to which we will all belong, and which will address all our needs for legality, training programs, civil liberties, etc. in a context of diversity and flexibility.

Part III: Qualifications and Functions of the Priesthood

(from *Green Egg*, Vol. 29, No. 116; Nov.-Dec. 1996)

WHAT ARE THE CRITERIA AND EXPECTATIONS FOR A PAGAN PRIESThood that might best serve our community? The qualities of Priesthood might be regarded in three categories: **Training, Service,** and **Character.** To address these areas, Pagan groups have developed Clergy training programs based upon the needs of their respective Traditions, Visions, and Missions. These range from the three-degree system of many Wiccan Traditions to the elaborate scholarly program of Ár nDraiocht Féin: A Druid Fellowship. The Aquarian Tabernacle Church, the Fellowship of Isis, the Henge of Keltria, the Ring of Troth, various Ceremonial Magick lodges, and other groups all have their own systems, with emphasis ranging from lore mastery and spellcraft to ritual adeptship and from individual psychic development to group leadership.

Although one may become a Priest or Priestess of a Deity merely be establishing and maintaining an altar or shrine to that Deity, and performing the appropriate rites, an ordained Priest or Priestess must also be in service to the Tribe. Within the Church of All Worlds there has been much discussion about what qualities, both tangible and intangible, might fulfill the needs of a Priesthood in our Church. Out of this we have developed our own training program for ordination and service as a CAW Priest or Priestess. These criteria are intended to be a guide for prospective candidates for ordination (Postulants) as well as for the continuing development of current members of the Priesthood. We do not, of course, expect that anyone would meet all these criteria perfectly, but rather that they should form a basis for expectations regarding one's Priestly functioning.

We are agreed, however, that fulfilling the criteria below is not enough, *in and of itself,* to warrant ordination. Knowledge is important, but there must also be significant internal growth that manifests consistently in actions and relationships. To achieve a balance between the logical linear sides of ourselves, our left brain functions, with the intuitive creative right brain functions, is a major necessity in becoming a Priest or Priestess. Therefore, we warn those seeking ordination that the internal work is just as important as the scholarly work. Postulants must be able to show, in their own way, what they have done in this area. Moreover, we expect our Priests and Priestesses to have their own lives in reasonable good order—substance addicts, Welfare dependents, prisoners, homeless, people whose personal relationships are in turmoil, etc. need to address these issues before they can expect to serve others!

With these caveats in mind, I offer this synopsis as an example of how this one Pagan church has conceptualized the role of a functioning Priesthood:

Training

- Active membership in this Church for at least three consecutive years, having served in the management of Church programs, functions and activities, as well as studies directed toward qualifying for Priesthood;
- Thorough familiarity with the Church and its subsidiary branches;
- Adequate religious/magickal training to show competency, leadership, and

originality. Studies should include as much as possible of the following subjects: mythology, cosmology, psychology, counseling, ecology, mysticism, divination, trance work, history, music, literature, theatre, comparative religion, theology, ritual design and construction, psychic development, healing, etc.

- Personal therapy as needed to clear out the cobwebs in the Postulant's personal life and history.
- An in-depth investigation of at least one other particular religious tradition. A study of particular healing traditions with a spiritual focus could also suffice.
- Have intimate familiarity with the Earth in Her more natural forms, including the ability to survive in relative wilderness, with at least a minimum of country and camping skills. This would be demonstrated by undertaking a solitary Vision Quest of at least three days and nights duration;
- Learn to create and lead effective rituals, ceremonies, rites of passage, events and meetings;
- Develop skills in mediation and conflict resolution;
- Have a charisma and sense of presence that is inspiring to others;
- Have personal credibility through integrity and lack of hypocrisy;
- Be authoritative, but not authoritarian;
- Be able to think on your feet and "wing it" when necessary;
- Be able to effectively lead others using "power with" instead of "power over;" know how to delegate;
- Be able to deal with administrative issues effectively, appropriately, and timely;
- Be able to raise power magically—to "carry the current."

Service-I

As for how Priests and Priestesses of the CAW are expected to function in their Priestly capacity, the following points are adapted from the CAW Member Handbook:

- Establish a link between the Gods and the community, and help people make that link themselves;
- Find joy in serving others;
- Administer the sacraments to the public as well as to CAW members. This may include pastoral counseling; ministering to the ill and dying; hospital and prison visitations; sitting with the bereaved; creating and performing rituals such as handfastings, baby blessings, coming-of-age rites, initiations, last rites, etc.;
- Articulately communicate the body of lore and teachings of the Church to anyone, through writing articles, giving interviews, teaching, magickal training, and ecological and political activities. Teach what you know—and know what you teach;
- Create original material;
- Take responsibility to make things happen;
- Put out fires effectively; mediate disputes and help resolve conflicts;
- Effectively lead others using "power with" instead of "power over;"
- Evoke a sense of affection and respect from others;
- Maintain clarity of Vision for the community;
- Deal with administrative issues effectively, appropriately, and timely;
- Lead regular services.

Service-II

(March 18, 1976; revised & updated Aug. 26, 1994; April 24. 2009; Feb. 9, 2012)

Here is an outline of the types of service to the community that Pagan Clergy may be expected to provide. The Priests and Priestesses ordained during CAW's 3rd phase (1978-2002) did (and still do) all of these things:

A. Personal service.
    1. Pastoral Counseling.
        a) individual counseling and therapy
        b) group counseling and mediation
        c) conflict resolution
        d) sensitivity sessions
        e) encounter groups
        f) psychedelic voyages
    2. Magickal/Religious Services and Sacraments.
        a) blessings
        b) weddings/handfastings
        c) funerals/memorial services
        d) exorcisms/cleansings
        e) initiations

B. Developing a Nest.
    1. Arranging meetings.
        a) open
        b) closed
    2. Creating and conducting events.
        c) rituals
        d) study programs
        e) classes and workshops
    3. Staging Sabbat festivals.
    4. Group outings and field trips.
    5. Group dynamics.

C. Public relations work.
    1. Public celebrations, presentations and demonstrations.
        a) lectures, presentations and workshops
        b) public rituals
    2. Giving interviews (radio, TV, newspapers, magazines, e-zines, blogs, etc.)
        a) friendly media
        b) hostile media
    3. Writing articles.
        a) Pagan, feminist, fan and other amateur "zines"
        b) slick publications
        c) blogs

D. Developing new programs and facets (eg: Lifeways, Forever Forests, *Green Egg,* Nemeton, ERA, HOME, POEM, Red Pentacles, *Book of Shadows,* tapes & CDs...)

By Daniel Blair Stewart

Service-III

A passage in Joan Grant's past-life novel, *Lord of the Horizon,* states very eloquently the essential character of one who would be a true Priest or Priestess:

> One who claims that he is more than ordinary men because he cannot be influenced by pleasures or discomforted by pain; who must be over-particular about his diet lest the fibers of his soul become coarsened; who must either remain immobile so that his vital energies may be conserved by meditation, or else must take excessive exertion so that his body is too weary to make any claim on his attention: such a man is not a priest, even though he may possess certain powers by which the credulous are easily impressed.
>
> But when you meet one to whom you can say, "you are my brother; you are a man as I am. Yesterday you were weak as I am weak, but now you are a little stronger than I and so can tell me how I too can grow." If you can say to him, "If we were to drink wine together we should both name the same vintage as the best; and if there was a choice of twenty meats, we should both fill our food-bowl from the same dish; and the women we love might be twin sisters." If you can say to him, "That which I suffer you have suffered also. You are close to me; you are my friend. You are ordinary as I am ordinary, and that is why you can understand why I am unhappy and know what has caused my unhappiness. Yesterday you were in sorrow, as I am now: but you found a cure of sorrow and that cure shall be mine also—for are we not brothers?"
>
> And if he, whom you call brother, is given that name also by the thief and by the cripple, by him who is betrayed and by the betrayer; by the concubine, by the wife, by the Overseer and by the beggar—then he has another name as well as Brother…That so ordinary man is a True Priest.
>
> ~Joan Grant, *Lord of the Horizon.* Avon, 1943

Of course, all this may be said as well of a true Priestess! One must be a part *of* the community, not apart *from* them. As the chant goes: "Of the People I do be, and the People part of me…" If the Tribe does not feel this kinship with those aspiring to be Priests or Priestesses, training is sterile and service is unacceptable. Priesthood can only function within the love and trust of a community devoted to a common Vision. Therefore, we in the CAW feel that the most important criterion for ordination is the *development of a constituency.* In order to be ordained, a Postulant must have a group of people who are willing to say: "We accept this person as *our* Priest/ess."

And in any magickal tradition, the people at its core must be in an extraordinary rapport of trust and love. We who are the Priests and Priestesses of the Church of All Worlds are held together by bonds of water shared. Anyone entering this inner Circle must, finally, be accepted by all of us into that intimate Water-Brotherhood of shared lives and purpose committed to our sacred destiny.

May You Never Thirst!

6. 99 Inherent Characteristics-Skills of a Priestess-Priest

(Author unknown)

ONE OF THE FIRST THINGS TO UNDERSTAND ABOUT PURSUING THE path of Priesthood, or answering the call to become a Priest/ess, is that it is a lot of work and not for everyone. Read the inherent characteristics of a Priestess or Priest listed below.

99 Inherent characteristics/skills of a Priestess/Priest:

1. Sees, envisions the big picture
2. Focuses on the future
3. Sets the vision
4. Displays a strong business acumen
5. Is not afraid to Set the direction
6. Strives for continuous improvement
7. Sees a cross-functional, cross-organizational view
8. Thinks critically
9. Focuses on the recipient
10. Possesses strong interpersonal skills
11. Communicates with transparency
12. Sends clear messages
13. Speaks in an impactful way
14. Gives open, honest, and direct feedback
15. Listens to understand people
16. Asks the right questions at the right time
17. Can break down complex information into simple terms
18. Interacts comfortably with people at all levels
19. Stays positive and constructive during difficult conversations
20. Finds middle ground and a path forward
21. Manages crisis and conflict with ease
22. Goes above and beyond
23. Focuses on results
24. Likes to succeed
25. Drives results
26. Gets things done
27. Stays goal-oriented and solution-focused
28. Acts decisively
29. Makes decisions in times of ambiguity
30. Completes difficult tasks despite obstacles
31. Exudes energy and determination
32. Pushes for what she or he believes in
33. Embodies a positive attitude
34. Has tenacity and curiosity
35. Strives to accomplish what they commit to doing
36. Takes ownership
37. Takes charge and assumes responsibility
38. Sets high standards
39. Has excellent organizational and execution skills
40. Embraces change and course-corrects when needed
41. Is fearless
42. Exudes passion, honesty, and dependability
43. Wins trust
44. Collaborates
45. Operates with integrity and fairness
46. Has a thirst for learning
47. Shares know-how
48. Shows empathy/sympathy
49. Is supportive and caring
50. Stays calm in difficult situations

51. Possesses leadership presence
52. Leads by example
53. Serves as a role model
54. Earns the respect of people at all levels of the organization
55. Stands up for what they believe in
56. Is an influencer
57. Inspires and empowers others
58. Motivates others during times of uncertainty
59. Influences without authority
60. Works across functions to get the job done
61. Manages up, down, and across
62. Engages differing points of view
63. Builds teams and fosters teamwork
64. Instills a sense of community
65. Adapts their message to the environment
66. Rallies people to achieve a common goal
67. Creates a shared sense of purpose
68. Relates work to the organization's goals to inspire action
69. Motivates people and aligns them around community goals
70. Ensures community spirit is upbeat
71. Is able to build collaborative teams and guides them to execute on big projects
72. Inspires people to act and move toward goals
73. Delegates
74. Sets clear expectations
75. Trusts others to do their jobs without micromanaging
76. Enables others to be successful
77. Removes obstacles from a team's path
78. Gives positive and constructive feedback
79. Allows people to learn from mistakes
80. Develops strong talent
81. Mentors, coaches, and develops people
82. Empowers others
83. Provides people with the tools and autonomy to get things done

84. Acts as a strong advocate for those they manage and mentor
85. Gives credit where it is due
86. Celebrates others' achievements
87. Rewards good performance
88. Creates opportunities for visibility
89. Attributes successes to those who contributed
90. Builds up team members and helps them grow
91. Understands the motivations of others to inspire them in their work
92. Identifies and utilizes others' strengths
93. Encourages others to do their best
94. Cares about the well-being of the community/Church
95. Enjoys seeing others succeed
96. Brings out the best in people
97. Helps others shine
98. Shows love and dedication in everything they do
99. Doesn't "throw" their "weight" around Reflect

Sit and Meditate on this list for 3 nights.
 1st - Focus on and highlight your strengths.
 2nd - What do you have to offer; which of these traits will you be able to utilize and teach to others?
 3rd - Which traits do you have room to grow within yourself?
 4th - Be honest, where are your shortcomings?

After you have reflected for 3 nights and journaled your responses to the 4 questions, sit again, and reflect deeply. Always hold in your heart the truth; there are a lot of different ways other than being a Priest/ess that you can show up for your community and your Church. Ask yourself these questions: Why do I want to be a Priest/ess? Will I be able to dedicate myself to selfless service? Is this the Path I choose?

7. CAW Canon Law on Clergy

Canon V: HIERARCHY AND COUNCILS

5.1. **Primate.** The Founder shall serve as Primate of the Church, being the sole and ultimate ecclesiastical authority, with powers to overrule any other official within the Church as to ecclesiastical matters, except when:

> **5.1.1.** The Primate dies, is removed from office or declared incompetent as detailed in Canons 6.4.4-6.4.5;
>
> **5.1.2.** Such action would be inconsistent with other Canons as set forth herein.

5.2. **Clergy Council.** Licensed Ministers, Priors, Prioresses, and members of the Priesthood (as defined in Canon X), combined shall constitute the Clergy Council, which shall function in the interests of the Church in such matters as cannot conveniently be brought before a regular or special meeting of the general membership or Scion Council.

> **5.2.1.** **Representation on Scion Council.** The Clergy Council shall have one representative sit on each meeting of the Scion Council as Counselor.
>
> **5.2.2.** **High Priest & Priestess.** The Clergy Council shall elect, from among the Priesthood, one member to serve as High Priest and one member to serve as High Priestess, who shall jointly chair the Council and stand to the laity as representatives of the Clergy.
>
> **5.2.3.** **Clergy Retreats.** At least annually a tribe-wide gathering of all Clergy shall be held for faith, friendship, enrichment, interaction, and communication. All Clergy and candidates shall be invited and are strongly encouraged to attend. Branches and regions may arrange similar retreats at a local level. A Clergy retreat special fund may be established and managed by the Treasurer of the Corporation to facilitate participation in these retreats.
>
> > **5.2.3.1.** Lay Attendance at Clergy Retreats. By special invitation, Clergy aspirants, inquirers, lay members of the church, and others may attend Clergy conferences provided their numbers do not distract from the fellowship and Clergy communication goals of the conference.
>
> **5.2.4.** **Conflict Resolution.** The Clergy Council shall be the body primarily responsible for defining and overseeing the process of formal conflict resolution used within CAW. The Clergy Council shall be empowered to establish a formal conflict resolution team, and shall oversee training and proper operation of any conflict resolution tasks.

5.3. **Priesthood Council.** Ordained members of the Priesthood, jointly met in council, shall constitute the Priesthood Council. This Council shall advance the vision and spiritual direction of the Church. This Council shall meet as a body at least once a year.

5.3.1.   **RINGS Oversight.** The Priesthood Council, or its delegated authority, shall determine the qualifications for advancement inward through the First and Second Rings, and shall fulfill any other such functions as shall be designated by the Primate, and may hold such regular or special meetings as shall be found necessary to adequately carry out the purposes of the Church.

Canon X: CLERGY

10.1.   **Religious Service.** While the program of progressive involvement in the tribe provides for many levels of service to the Divine, to the Church, to the Mission of CAW and to the Curia (Waterkin tribe) of CAW, some members of the Church of All Worlds are called to a life of more intense dedication and service to the Divine, the Church, and humanity. After proper training, reflection, and vision questing, these persons may be received into the Clergy by way of ordination (Priesthood) or Ministerial licensure.

10.2.   **Priesthood:** Some of those persons are called to a ministry of sacramental service to the Divine, celebrating the Rites and Rituals of the Church of All Worlds and representing the Church in a consistent manner. Upon application and due consideration by the Priesthood Council, these persons may be received into the Priesthood by the sacrament of ordination.

10.2.1.   **Duties.** Duties of the Priesthood shall include providing spiritual guidance and counsel to other members, hosting and officiating at various ceremonies and services, administering the sacraments, writing and preparing rituals, participating in the Clergy and Priesthood Councils, supervising the training of Seekers and Scions, sponsoring and aiding postulants to the Priesthood, serving as conscience dictates, and if duly elected, as members of the Board of Directors, facilitating communications among Nests, and any other such duties as may be determined by the Priesthood Council.

10.2.2.   **Ordination.** Ordination into the Priesthood may be bestowed upon members who have completed all the currently-stated qualifications of Priesthood, who have been recommended for ordination by any sponsoring member of the Priesthood, and have been approved unanimously by the Priesthood Council through the submission of such data as they may choose to require.

10.2.3.   **High Priest and High Priestess.** The titles "High Priest" and High Priestess" are honorific and may be applied to only one man and/or one woman at a time (ideally one of each). These are religious titles granted in recognition of such individuals as the foremost Clergy representatives of the Church and are meant primarily to denote such status in interactions outside the Church, such as interfaith conferences and forums, public interviews and media presentations, etc. where it is appropriate to have the Church's authorized representatives designated by suitable titles of rank.

10.2.3.1. Qualifications. To qualify for the title of High Priest or High Priestess, said individual must be a superb ritualist and public speaker, and be acknowledged High Priest or High Priestess by the Priesthood Council. He or she should have served on the Board of Directors.

10.2.3.2. Duties. The primary duties of the High Priest and High Priestess shall be to co-chair the Priesthood Council and to be a Clergy representative and ambassador of CAW to the outside world.

10.2.3.3. Term of Office. The title of High Priest or High Priestess may be held for no longer than seven years in succession, during which time it shall be the duty of said persons to select and train their successors. If at any time no member of the Priesthood is qualified, acknowledged, or willing to hold one of these titles, said title shall languish until an appropriate recipient arises.

10.2.3.4. Co-Equal with Other Clergy. While the High Priest and High Priestess serve as facilitators for the Clergy Council and present the face of the Clergy to the outside world as the representatives of the Church, they are nevertheless considered to be co-equal to all other members of the Priesthood.

10.3. Ministers. Individuals who desire to serve in a less ambitious Clergy capacity than Priesthood may be approved and licensed as Ministers and issued Ministerial Credentials. Licensed CAW Ministers shall function as the equivalent of Chaplains, and be authorized to perform such sacraments as authorized by the Priesthood Council. In order to qualify for this special status, the postulant must submit a Ministerial Application to the Priesthood Council indicating the nature of the intended Ministry and his/her qualifications to fulfill it.

10.3.1. Clergy, not Priesthood. Ministers shall be regarded as Clergy, but not as part of the Priesthood, which is a designation reserved for ordained Priests & Priestesses.

10.3.2. Ministry. A Minister may form his/her ministry as a subordinate organization subject to the provisions of Canon 14.

10.4. Priories. A Scion of 6th Circle or inward may be appointed by the Priesthood Council to be a spiritual steward for Sacred Land involving a Temple or a community of votaries. Such person may be nominated by their community and shall be installed as a Prior or Prioress whose duties shall include administrative and ministerial functions to be determined by the Priesthood Council or their delegated authority.

> **10.4.1. Clergy, not Priesthood.** Priors/Prioresses shall be regarded as Clergy, but not as part of the Priesthood, which is a designation reserved for ordained Priests & Priestesses.

Priestess Morning Glory & Priest Oberon Zell, October 1973.

8.Clergy Status Definitions

"Active" = Membership active and in good standing, actively participating in the life of CAW (Inc.) as a Church.

"Inactive" = Membership may be active or may have lapsed; member does not meet the requirements of an active participant or paid dues for a period of a year and a day, has not notified the respective Council of his/her intent and has not requested leave.

"On Sabbatical" = Membership may be active or may have lapsed, but otherwise in good standing, not actively participating in the life of the Church due to personal reasons (health, family, employment, in school, etc.).

"Probationary" = Membership active, returned or returning to the Church; has applied for but has not yet completed the RINGS reinstatement process. Completing their 6 month "reconnection" requirement, or plan of action to meet new RINGS requirements. Treated as "active" for most purposes.

"CAW Tradition" = May or may not currently be a dues-paying member of CAW, but is continuing to serve the CAW Community as a member of the Priesthood/Clergy/Beacon or Scion in a CAW Tradition. **NOT** legally connected to CAW, not responsible to CAW, Inc. or bound by CAW, Inc. ethics, guidelines, By-Laws, Canons, procedures or policies and CAW, Inc. is not legally liable in any way for their beliefs or actions.

"Retired" = May or may not currently be a member of CAW, Inc. but is not currently functioning within CAW as a member of the Priesthood. As with CAW Tradition members, except that they may or may not be serving the community as a member of the Priesthood/Clergy/Beacon or Scion, and may or may not consider themselves a member of a CAW Tradition. Retired members who advise us that they are serving the CAW community within the CAW Tradition may be listed as CAW Tradition Priesthood if they so desire.

"Resigned" = Voluntarily disassociated from their position without prejudice. Member may still retain CAW membership, but does not perform any duties of their Clergy position.

"Defrocked" = Involuntarily disassociated from CAW due to unacceptable behavior or ethics. Members who are "defrocked" may have their membership revoked and may even be banned from returning as members.

9. High Priestess of CAW

By Anodea Judith, *March 13, 1998*

I HELD THE TITLE OF HIGH PRIESTESS OF CHURCH OF ALL WORLDS for approximately ten years. Seven of those years I was President ("Presitess"), and the remaining three, I kept on as HPs by request of the Clergy Council and general membership. At that time, CAW was the center of my life, and I was conducting rituals, teaching classes, involved with CAW administration, writing, traveling, etc. CAW also flourished and grew tremendously during that time.

When I set down the mantle as CAW HPs, I passed it on to Morning Glory, as she was the senior priestess member of the Clergy Council. She took it dubiously, but agreed she was the most appropriate person at the time. I trust and respect MG's magical sensibilities, even if I don't agree with her on all issues. She is an active member in the Clergy, traveling frequently t o the rest of the world. She groks CAW pretty thoroughly.

I believe the office of High Priestess is a magical office, not a political one, and an extremely important one in a magical organization. Though each member of a circle in a given ritual is part of the magick, contributing and making it happen, connecting to the gods, etc., having a designated priest and/or priestess of the circle helps the circle remain focused and potent. This person is not better than the rest, just the one designated to gather and focus the threads of energy that are woven into a coherent creation. This is much like a conductor of an orchestra, coordinating everyone's magical efforts.

I believe the office of a CAW High Priestess, held by a single qualified female member of the Clergy, is also a necessary one. While each member, Scion, Clergy, and Nest has the ability to interface directly with the gods in their own way, and weave their own magic, I believe the magical coherence of CAW as an organization is or should be held and woven together on the psychic planes by the current HPs, in conjunction with other members of the Clergy, Nest leaders, Scions, and general membership.

However, a leaderless circle is better than a circle lead by chaos, or led by one who is not able to do it well.

I believe we should keep the office of HPs in the Canons, but state that it is appointed by the Clergy Council by acclamation of the general membership. I believe the term should be 3-7 years, with a one-year probationary first term. If there is no one who can carry this role willingly and effectively, I believe the office should remain empty, and we should try not having one, until someone suitable steps forward. But I believe that to do away with the role altogether will court chaos. The more we fight coordination, the more uncoordinated we will become.

I believe the matter should be decided by unanimous vote of the Clergy Council, based on suggestions made by the general membership and the Council's general understanding of the magic at the time.

HPs Job Description

I believe the job description of High Priestess is a difficult one. Here are some of the duties I performed:

1. Coordinate the Clergy Council and keep it magically connected.
2. Assist in the training of Clergy and membership.
3. Be a part of or consultant in major CAW rituals (such as Beltaines, Samhains, Mysteries, or festival rituals).
4. Travel to the general public and interface with other members, Nests, and the world at large.
5. Be exemplary in one's actions, worthy of respect from the outside world.
6. Hold a basic set of CAW tools to guard over, and keep a special altar just for the Church itself.
7. Write a column in *Scarlet Flame* that will give us magical focus and tell us what's up between this world and the other.

CAW Grand Reunion at Heartland Pagan Festival, 1990. Left front, **OZ.** Kneeling behind banner: **Orion Stormcrow, Tom Kullman, Mark Kullman,** *Wayne Ochs, Ed Short II.* Directly behind them: *Don Wildgrube, Carolyn Clark,* **Tom Williams.** Back row, L-R: **Anodea Judith,** *Morning Glory, Fred Buck,* **Tzipora Katz, Annie Heartsong,** *Steve Frischer, Jim Ware (Morgyn), Spencer Knapp,* **Howard Nelson, D.J. Hamouris,** *LaRue & Lance Christie,* **Cary Robyn** (photographer). In very back with a white hat, **Jim Chamberlain.** Right front, *Diane Darling, Oberon the Faerie Unicorn. (Italics = deceased)*

10. The Perfect High Priestess!

(Author unknown)

THE PERFECT HIGH PRIESTESS' CIRCLES ARE ALWAYS ON TIME, AND run exactly 20 minutes. She is deeply devoted to her tutelary Goddess, but never belittles other people's gods, not even the Sacred Sky Bunny. She works from 6:00 am until midnight, and also sweeps up after circle and carries out the garbage.

The Perfect High Priestess excels in a demanding professional career, and donates all her time to community concerns. She came from humble origins and is always happy for a crust of bread, a rind of cheese, or a place on your sofa while she is on lavish book tours for her publisher, Harper Collins.

She has a big comfortable home which she always makes available to the community, and spends most of her time in study and personal work. She is quiet and unpretentious, she blends into the background, and her experience and power are apparent to anyone who meets her.

She cares nothing for appearances, wears good clothes, drives a good car, buys and loans out good books, and donates candles, altar cloths and incense to the coven. She is 39 years old and has 40 years' experience in a previous life. Above all, she is beautiful and of course she is female.

The Perfect High Priestess has a burning desire to work with novices, and she spends most of her time with an authentic traditional coven. Her coven, which upholds the old customs of secrecy, is known and respected on several continents. She can be trusted with any private confidence, and is a generous fount of knowledge, on procedures, people, and the gossip of the Craft, dating back to when Gerald was just back from Burma.

She smiles all the time with a straight face because she has a sense of humor that keeps her seriously dedicated to her Craft. She always attends local coffee cauldrons, festivals, and workshops, and is always by the phone to be handy when needed. Unfortunately, most Perfect High Priestesses are always in another city!

If your High Priestess does not measure up, simply send this notice to six other covens that are tired of their High Priestess, too. Then bundle up your High Priestess and send her to the coven at the top of your list. If everyone cooperates, in one month you will receive 1,643 High Priestesses. One of them should be perfect.

Have faith in this letter. Don't break the chain! One coven broke the chain and got its old High Priestess back in less than three months, along with Lance Spearshaft, a new male lover she picked up in Vegas. Lance proceeded to beguile several women in the coven before running off with their BoS, $827 in IOU's, and the coven Maiden. Don't let it happen to you!

11. Pagan Clergy Code of Conduct

By Angie Buchanan
(Adapted for CAW from the Earth Traditions Ministry Training Program)
http://www.earthtraditions.org/training.htm

Note from Angie Buchanan, founder of Earth Traditions Ministry:
Sent: Tuesday, December 27, 2011 2:26 PM
Subject: RE: Earth Traditions Ministry Training
Hi Oberon,
You have my permission to use the ETMT Code of Conduct for your own training purposes.
I'm really not familiar with any good books on Pagan Clergy - which is partially why we began this program. Perhaps we'll write one!
Love, ~Angie

IN ISSUING THIS CODE, WE WOULD LIKE TO CONFIRM OUR STRONG personal commitment to the bond of trust between the Clergy of the Church of All Worlds and the Pagan community in general. We are all here to serve and we must serve honestly and in the interests of those who give us their trust.

We expect all CAW Clergy to work within the letter and spirit of the Code. It is our hope that our Clergy will find it a useful source of guidance and reference as they undertake their official duties in a way that upholds the highest standards of propriety.

Responsibility

We believe we should be absolutely clear about how Clergy should account, and be held accountable by their peers and the communities they serve.

The public and private conduct of Clergy has the ability to inspire and motivate people, but it can also alienate and undermine. CAW Clergy must, at all times, be aware of the sacred responsibilities that accompany their calling. "With great power comes great responsibility." (—Stan Lee, *Spiderman*)

Responsibility for adherence to the Code of Conduct rests with the individual. CAW Clergy need to have an understanding that their personal lives and behaviors do affect the group and organization.

Corrective action may take various forms—from a verbal reproach to revocation of credentials—depending on the specific nature and circumstances of the offense and the extent of the harm.

Clergy Standards

This Clergy Code of Conduct is in no way intended to define the experiences a Priest or Priestess has in their personal life. However; it is vitality important that one who uses the titles of Clergy, Minister, Priest or Priestess possess a clear understanding of the very real and complicated issues involved. The effect on both individual and community must be considered when assessing the safe and appropriate ethics. Significant thought, introspection and consultation with peers should be sought to ensure that any potential harm to others has been assessed and avoided when conducting Clergy duties and conducting work that represents the Church of All Worlds. The following applies to conduct affected within the confines of the role of Clergy.

Clergy Conduct when serving as Pastoral Counselors and Spiritual Directors

When one is serving in the role of Spiritual Director or Pastoral Counselor, they are engaged in the various duties associated with Clergy practice. These duties include but are not limited to facilitation of rituals, teaching, planning for and performing Rites of Passage, participation in the interfaith and intrafaith arenas, staffing events, etc.

1. Clergy serving as Pastoral Counselors and Spiritual Directors must respect the rights and advance the welfare of each person.
2. Clergy serving as Pastoral Counselors or Spiritual Directors shall not step beyond their competence in counseling or in other areas instead, will refer clients to the appropriate professionals or resources as needed.
3. Clergy serving as Pastoral Counselors or Spiritual Directors should carefully consider the possible consequences before entering into a counseling or ministerial relationship with someone with whom they have a pre-existing relationship (i.e., employee, professional colleague, friend, or other pre-existing relationship).
4. Clergy serving as Pastoral Counselors or Spiritual Directors should not audiotape or videotape sessions.
5. Clergy must never engage in sexual intimacies with the persons they counsel professionally.
6. Clergy serving as Pastoral Counselors or Spiritual Directors assume the full burden of responsibility for establishing and maintaining clear, appropriate boundaries in all counseling and counseling-related relationships.
7. Sessions should not be held at places or times that would tend to cause confusion about the nature of the relationship for the person being counseled or other observers.
8. Clergy serving as Pastoral Counselors or Spiritual Directors shall maintain a log of the times and places of sessions with each person counseled.

Confidentiality

While Clergy are not bound by the same ethical standards as therapists, it may be that in the act of Pastoral Counseling the individual may assume that you are going to hold their self-disclosure in confidence. It is expected that as the Pastoral Counselor you will set the boundaries and seek the necessary clarification about the need and desire for confidentiality. It is also essential that if for whatever reason you do not feel you can maintain confidentiality that you state that as soon as possible and directly to the individual involved.

1. Information disclosed to a Pastoral Counselor during the course of counseling, advising, or spiritual direction shall be held in the strictest confidence possible.
2. Information obtained in the course of sessions shall be confidential, except for compelling professional reasons or as required by law.
3. If there is clear and imminent danger to the client or to others, the Pastoral Counselor may disclose only the information necessary to protect the parties affected and to prevent harm.
4. Before disclosure is made, if feasible, the Pastoral Counselor should inform the person being counseled about the disclosure and the potential consequences.
5. Pastoral Counselors should discuss the nature of confidentiality and its limits with each person in counseling.
6. Pastoral Counselors should keep minimal records of the content of sessions, if any record is necessary.
7. Knowledge that arises from professional contact may be used in teaching, writing, or other public presentations only when effective measures are taken to absolutely safeguard both the individual's identity and the confidentiality of the disclosures.
8. While counseling a minor, if a Pastoral Counselor discovers that there is a serious threat to the welfare of the minor and that communication of confidential information to a parent or legal guardian is essential to the child's health and wellbeing, the Counselor or Spiritual Director should:
   - Attempt to secure written consent from the minor for the specific disclosure.
   - If consent is not given, disclose only the information necessary to protect the health and wellbeing of the minor.

Conduct with Youth

Clergy, when working with youth, shall maintain an open and trustworthy relationship between youth and themselves.

1. Clergy must be aware of their own and others' vulnerability when working alone with youth. Use a team approach to managing youth activities.
2. Physical contact with youth can be misconstrued and should occur (a) only when completely nonsexual and otherwise appropriate (such as hugging), and (b) never in private.
3. Clergy should review and know the contents of the child abuse regulations and reporting requirements for the state in which they reside and work, and should follow those mandates.

Sexual Conduct

Clergy must not, for sexual gain or intimacy, exploit the trust placed in them by the community.

1. No CAW Clergy may exploit another person for sexual purposes.
2. Clergy must be aware at all times of the image that they are portraying and be cognizant of the perceptions that are sending. Expressions of sensuality can be used

as positive metaphors however; the need to be aware of potential misrepresentations are the responsibly of the Clergy. Action must be taken to be clear about your intentions and assessing any potential damage of said expressions.

3. Allegations of sexual misconduct shall be taken seriously and reported to the appropriate person and to civil authorities if the situation involves a minor or dependent person.

Harassment

Clergy must not engage in physical, psychological, written, or verbal harassment, and must not tolerate such harassment by others.

1. Harassment encompasses a broad range of physical, written, or verbal behavior, including without limitation the following:
   - Physical or mental abuse.
   - Derogatory ethnic or racial insults.
   - Unwelcome sexual advances or touching.
   - Requests for sexual favors, especially used as a condition of training, advancement, or ordination.
2. Harassment can be a single severe incident or a persistent pattern of behavior where the purpose or the effect is to create a hostile, offensive, or intimidating environment.

Conflict of Interest—Dual Relationships

In most community contexts, Clergy are required by their ethical and professional governing bodies to avoid engaging in dual or multiple role relationships. In other words, they are to endeavor to avoid becoming business partners, sexual partners, or even friends. Such dual relationships may engender complex entanglements and obligations that are not facilitative of effective counseling or ministry, bringing about conflicts of interest that make consideration of the best interests of a client or counselee very difficult.

Frequently however, Clergy find it difficult or impossible to avoid multiple relationships, particularly in small or close-knit religious communities. In such cases, Clergy must strive to be aware of and work to impose boundaries between personal life and professional life, between friendship and counseling roles.

They should seek supervision and peer consultation as a means of being accountable for decisions and choices, keeping firmly in mind the best interests of those whom they serve. In social situations in which they are called upon to exercise some aspect of their Clergy role, they should be conscious of professional comportment, appearance, and the impact of their actions on those with whom they work and the organization for whom they work.

Paganism is such a context in which dual relationships are difficult to avoid. Though growing in numbers in diverse place in the world, Pagans nevertheless have become remarkably close-knit. Pagan Clergy frequently find themselves in a position in which they are compelled to provide spiritual counseling to friends or coven mates. At gatherings or in other public contexts they may be called upon to act in accordance with their Clergy role, which may occasionally be at odds with personal inclinations, values, or activities. In such cases, mentoring relationships or consultations with Elders are critical for ethical and professional behavior and comportment that effectively balances the personal and professional.

1. The Church of All Worlds expects its Clergy to show professional comportment in public, self-awareness in private counseling, and a respectful willingness to engage in mentoring and peer consultation when necessary.
2. Clergy should not provide counseling services to any one with whom they have a business, professional, or social relationship. When this is unavoidable, the client must be protected. The counselor must establish and maintain clear, appropriate boundaries.
3. When pastoral counseling or spiritual direction services are provided to two or more people who have a relationship with each other, the counselor must:
   - Clarify with all parties the nature of each relationship,
   - Anticipate any conflict of interest,
   - Take appropriate actions to eliminate the conflict, and
   - Obtain from all parties written consent to continue services.
4. Conflicts of interest may also arise when a counselor's independent judgment is impaired by:
   - Prior dealings,
   - Becoming personally involved.

Stonehenge Eclipse, Maryhill, WA Feb. 28, 1979.

12. The Church of All Worlds Tradition

By Liza Gabriel, Oberon Zell, and Morning Glory Zell, 2002

I. The Future of the Church of All Worlds Tradition

AS FOUNDERS, ELDERS, AND LONG-TERM PRACTITIONERS OF THE Church of All Worlds, we have come together to celebrate and proclaim what we see all around us, that the practices, traditions, and values of the CAW are now a Tradition of Neo-Paganism, like Wicca, and no longer wholly centered in any one organization or under any one authority. We honor the contributions of the people who choose to be affiliated with the legally incorporated organization called Church of All Worlds, as well as all of those people who follow this Tradition and choose other affiliations—or no affiliation at all.

We proclaim this in affirmation and support of all who identify with the principles and practices of the Church of All Worlds Tradition, regardless of their chosen organizational affiliation. We wish everyone who wants to have a Nest of this Tradition, or to practice in this Tradition, or to build a new Church or other organization in this Tradition, to be empowered to do so; just as Wiccans and other Traditions have room for many expressions. We want everyone of this Tradition to feel free to express this Tradition in his or her own way, answering only to the authority, institution or organization that each individual feels truly called to.

We do this for the sake of clarity and empowerment of all people practicing and cherishing the Tradition of the Church of All Worlds and in honor of all the loving and caring contributions to this Tradition by people who may no longer identify with any particular organization. The Neo-Pagan religious movement is growing fast. Deep within in it is the founding and seminal influence of the Church of All Worlds and the generations of Pagan leaders it has produced. Let us rejoice in our diversity and celebrate our common heritage!

As free Practitioners of the Church of All Worlds Tradition, we proclaim these values and practices as central to our tradition and in so doing acknowledge every group and individual's freedom to interpret these and shape them to their current context. We do not know what contexts future generations will encounter!

After reading the statements below, we invite you to join us in affirming the beauty and magick of the Church of All Worlds Tradition and to empower all of its practitioners.

II. Basic Principles of the Church of All Worlds Tradition

The Church of All Worlds Tradition is an eclectic tradition of Neo-Paganism. Its practices are intended as a means towards the best outcome for all. The CAW Tradition is ever-evolving with basic, inclusive practices as follows:

Reverence for the Earth

Practitioners of the CAW Tradition revere, honor, and protect the Earth. Most believe that our planet is a conscious living being—Gaia, or Mother Earth. Most revere Her as a manifestation of the Great Mother Goddess worshipped by human beings from the dawn of time.

Immanent Divinity

Practitioners of the CAW Tradition honor the God and/or Goddess as immanent in every human being, voiced in the common greeting, "Thou Art God," or "Thou Art Goddess." The deepest experience of the Divinity in other people and things comes through the process of *grokking*. Literally, *grokking* means "drinking." In practice it means expanding ones identity to include the whole being of another person or thing.

Sharing Water

In harmony with the process of *grokking,* the water that is essential to all life is the primary Sacrament of the CAW Tradition. Water is Blessed and passed in a chalice, or otherwise shared. Often the last drops are offered to the Divine. Usually when a chalice is passed, the person passing blesses the person receiving the chalice by saying, "Never Thirst," "Thou Art God," "Drink Deep," "Don't spit in the cup," or other appropriate words. This ritual, more than any other, is the common practice of the CAW Tradition.

Water Kinship

The intention of the Water Sharing ritual is to affirm bonds of kinship. Depending on the intimacy of the circle, four levels of this bond are common:
1. Affirming our connection to each other and to all life;
2. Affirming belonging to a tribe or tradition;
3. Affirming friendship;
4. A lifelong Commitment of deep communion, friendship, love, and compassion, which may or may not have an erotic component.

Nests

Nests are the basic grouping of the Church of All Worlds Tradition and are composed of at least three people who have a consistent commitment to the Tradition. At least one member, the Nest Coordinator, should have at least one year experience and the blessing of other long-term practitioners of the Tradition. A Nest may begin with no experience and work towards the ideals of Nesthood. Some Nests are families. Others are social networks, or ritual working groups. They are usually small and intimate. Sometimes several Nests may form a Branch.

It is likely that the current legal organization called Church of All Worlds may choose not to recognize such Nests, Branches or the leadership status of these non-affiliated individuals or groups. Some unofficial Nests may choose to pursue affiliation with the legal organization at some point whereas others may choose to remain permanently unaffiliated.

Freedom of Expression in Intimacy & Family

The Church of All Worlds Tradition is associated with open attitudes towards intimacy and sexuality. How this is practiced differs widely from person to person and Nest to Nest. Practitioners of the CAW Tradition affirm and support the broadest diversity of intimate and familial expression consistent with a sustainable and ethical life. For example, CAW practitioners support same-sex bonding through marriage, handfasting or other means. While quite a number of practitioners of the CAW Tradition are monogamous, all support the full range of choice in relationship, including intimate relationships and familial bonds that contain more than two adults; in other words, polyamory.

A Tradition that Looks Equally to Future and Past

Four of the five practices above derive directly from *Stranger in a Strange Land*, the 1961 science fiction novel by Robert Heinlein in which the name "Church of All Worlds" first appeared. Some members of the CAW Tradition glow with pride over this fact, while others are embarrassed and do not wish to be identified with the book. There is no question that many aspects of the book are increasingly outdated.

What will never be outdated, however, is the Church of All World Tradition's embrace of the mythology of the future and of science and technology as sources of wisdom as valid as the sacred traditions of old. The CAW Tradition honors the ancient past and looks, with equal reverence, to the future.

Fun

Humor, enjoyment, play, fantasy, and all forms of pleasure are central to the ways that practitioners of the Church of All Worlds Tradition come together.

III. Practices of other Neo-Pagan Traditions shared in common by the CAW Tradition

1. **Polytheism.** Most practitioners of the CAW Tradition believe that Divinity takes many forms and worship whatever forms are meaningful to the individual. The Myths and Mysteries of many Deities provide deep sources of initiation and wisdom for practitioners of the Church of All World Tradition.

2. **The Wheel of the Year.** Like nearly all Pagan traditions, the CAW Tradition celebrates the cycles of the seasons, especially the traditional quarters and cross quarters: Ostara, Beltaine, Litha, Lughnasadh, Mabon, Samhain, Yule, and Oimelc/Imbolg.

3. **Magick.** Practitioners of the CAW Tradition may use traditional and untraditional means to influence the course of events through the focus of personal will. They acknowledge, honor and use unseen forces beyond rational human understanding.

4. **The Rede.** Most CAW practitioners support *the Wiccan Rede* as a foundation: 'An it harm none, do as you will.' However, in the CAW Tradition, it is understood that

all magic whether it serves personal ends or not is intended to move towards the best outcome for all. The CAW Tradition looks beyond the perennial spiritual value of non-harming, and actively contributes to the evolution of the whole. What form this takes varies widely.

5. **Casting a Circle.** Practitioners of the CAW Tradition frequently cast a circle by ritually drawing it with a blade, wand, or other power object. The circle then serves as a place of protection, holiness, and power in which religious and magical acts are accomplished. The ideal of every action and relationship inside the circle is *perfect love and perfect trust*.

6. **The Five Elements.** Practitioners of the CAW Tradition often use the traditional elements, Air, Fire, Water, Earth and Spirit and the corresponding directions East, South, West, North and Center as important parts of religious practice.

7. **Evoking the God and Goddess.** Practitioners of the CAW Tradition often choose individuals in their circles to serve as focal points and expressions of the Divine Male and Female. This is called *aspecting*. Divinity is also invited into the ritual circle on its own without being invited into a particular individual.

8. **Bardship.** The CAW Tradition is a rich source of song, chant, ritual, art, lore, scholarship, vision and so on. The practitioners of the CAW Tradition who have made major contributions to the creative life of the Neo-Pagan Movement and the broader culture are too numerous to name. Innovation and creativity are valued and nourished.

9. **Influences of Other Traditions.** The CAW Tradition enjoys and embraces influences from all the world's religions and traditions in ways that complement its basic principles and practices.

IV. Conclusion

Our recognition of a broader CAW Tradition is a positive acknowledgement of what already exists within the diverse spiritual spectrum of the Pagan Movement. As such it should be viewed as an attempt to reach beyond the status quo and to heal past rifts by creating a larger, more inclusive pattern of identification. In the past there have been many polarizing issues that have divided CAW. Perhaps this unorthodox form of recognition can encourage peaceful co-existence and give birth to an informal resolution of these conflicts since actual agreements are not a possibility at this point.

The skilled and wise practitioners of the Church of All Worlds Tradition are too numerous to count. We know that many of them will join us in this affirmation of our tradition and heritage, and in addition will teach, write, and create their visions, answering to their own authority in the freedom and embrace of our evolving Tradition. We are counting on these people to contribute their rich and diverse wisdom to the world for the good of all. Our hope is for a cooperative and diverse honoring of our common values, heritage and practices.

We thus declare: *Make It So!*

13. CAW Precepts

by Oberon Zell, Primate
(from *CAW Membership Handbook,* 3rd Edition, 1997)

NO MATTER HOW WE FORMULATE OUR PHILOSOPHY, THE TRUE TEST of our strength lies in our behavior—our ability to embody the principles we hold dear, and apply them in our daily lives to the building of relationships and community, the integrity of our actions, and the strength of character that inspires others to grow and transform the world around them. To these ends we advocate the following principles of behavior:

1. **Be Excellent to Each Other!** Thou Art God/dess. To truly honor the Divinity within each other is to treat each other with respect, kindness, courtesy, and conscious consideration. This involves honest and responsible communication, including the avoidance of gossip and rumor-mongering, and the willingness to reach for understanding rather than judgment. Learn how to communicate in a positive, life-affirming way. We prefer to avoid us/them and either/or thinking, and to instead take an inclusive systems approach that sees the Divinity in all living things. To this end we also deplore coercive behavior that does not respect the free will of others. We prefer to lead, not by guilt or coercion, but by inspiration and example; not only to be excellent to each other, but to strive for excellence in all our endeavours, no matter how seemingly insignificant. Tribal values we hold include Loyalty, Generosity, Fairness and Hospitality.

2. **Be Excellent to Yourself!** Again: Thou Art God/dess. Divinity resides within as well as without, so how you treat yourself is how you treat that Divinity. Self-abuse, whether through irresponsible use of substances, overwork, self-denial, self-deception, or simply running those tapes that undermine self-esteem, are all insults to the Divinity within. Treat yourself kindly, with compassion rather than judgment, and it will be easier to treat others that way. Take care of your body, home and possessions, as a piece of Gaia that has been entrusted to you. Be a conscious guardian to the Temple and the God/dess within.

3. **Honor Diversity!** In Nature a diverse ecosystem has more stability. There are many styles of living and ways of living, each of which has something to offer to the overall puzzle of life. Be open-minded and receptive to new ideas because this usually manifests in growth of the spirit and the mind. Learn about differences rather than judge them. Be willing to explore others' creative abilities to manifest a sense of well-being and confidence in their own Divinity. Sexism, racism, or rude remarks directed towards other's sexual preferences, body type or personal habits (insofar as they do not harm others) have no place in this community. **All life is sacred.**

4. **Take Personal Responsibility!** ("With great power comes great responsibility!") The necessary counterpart to individual freedom is the willingness to be personally responsible for all of our actions, and for our effects upon the planet. Only through

the practice of personal responsibility can we become responsible collectively and live a life of freedom and maturity. We are not a religion of gurus, Mommies or Daddies who can tell you what to do. As a religion that respects equality, we must take equal responsibility for making things happen, preventing harm, or cleaning up mistakes. To this end we also advocate one of the principles taught in kindergarten; **Clean up your mess!**

5. **Consider the Consequences!** What is it that distinguishes wisdom from foolishness? Simple. Wisdom is about seeing the larger picture, and considering the consequences of every word and deed. Foolishness is what happens when we pursue our own narrow self-interest and ignore any consideration of consequences. To see sterling examples of this, just observe most politicians in action!

6. **Walk Your Talk!** (and talk your walk!) Talk is cheap. It is fine and well to proclaim to be a feminist or environmentalist, to preach heady Pagan gospel, or to play holier than thou. It is only in practice that words become Truth, and change becomes manifest. But do not be afraid to fail, for in order to grow, our reach must exceed our grasp, and it is through failing that we learn.

14. Sexual Etiquette

By Morning Glory Zell, High Priestess

UNITY THROUGH DIVERSITY IS A FOUNDING TENET OF THE CHURCH of All Worlds; because of this, not everyone's idea of acceptable behavior is the same. So to avoid undue stress, confusion, and bad vibes, here are some reminders:

1. **Sexuality and the Sacred Freedom** thereof is one of our prime values, so respect it. ("All acts of love and pleasure are My rituals.") Sexual activities that are engaged in by informed and mutually-consenting adults are *no one else's business,* and are not to be condemned or censured. By the same token, it is *absolutely unacceptable* to attempt to pressure, cajole or coerce another into any sexual activity that they do not wish freely and wholeheartedly to participate in.

2. **Minor issues.** While the respect due sacred sexuality applies *in principle* to Pagans of all ages, the emotional as well as legal pitfalls involved make it imperative that adults absolutely avoid sexually-charged interaction with youths below the legal age of consent. There are specific laws concerning age, although Clergy are not mandated reporters.

3. **Be sure you interpret signals correctly.** A loving touch, hug or a massage is not an invitation to coitus, so if your attempts at intimacy or caring make someone uncomfortable, *stop!* And if someone touches you in an uncomfortable fashion, ***tell them!*** If that doesn't work, get a Priestess, Priest, or Festival staff member to help you. Please be sensitive as to how your affections are perceived/received.

4. **Practice safe sex!** Use condoms with all outside your Condom Compact; and if you have an STD (Sexually Transmitted Disease), *tell your consort.*

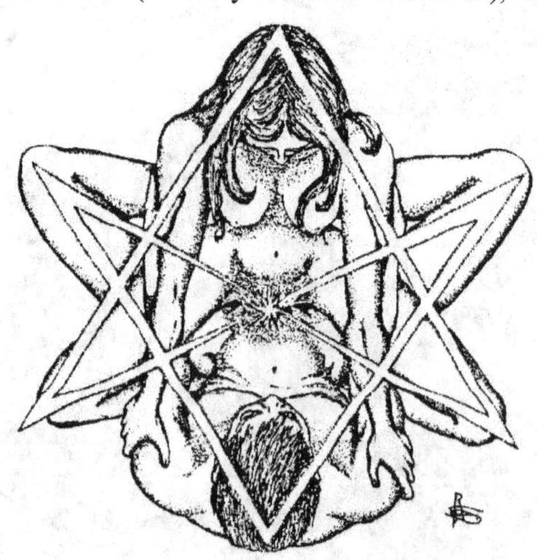

Sex Magick by Nema.

15. Sacred Sexuality and Sacred Services in CAW

By Francesca Gentille

CAW CLERGY IN NO WAY CERTIFIES OR PROVIDES ANY SEXUAL services. However, if Sacred Sexuality and Sacred Service of that type is part of your personal practice, we have the following suggestions and expectations for etiquette and safety. We expect everyone to practice the absolute highest degree of Consent.

Bringing Sexuality and the Sacred together can be a powerful and beautiful healing experience for all involved. And, all who practice it need to be aware of the inherent risk for harm as well. In order to ensure that, as Clergy, we follow the Rede and harm none, bringing Consent and mindfulness to any Sacred Sexuality interaction is essential.

NOTE: Any Sacred Sexual interaction must include setting a magickal container and having clear intention for each interaction.

What is Sacred Sexuality?

"All acts of love and pleasure are my Rituals"

Bringing Magick into sexuality is something that all Pagans may do as part of their personal practice if they are so inclined and do so with Consent. However, any Priesthood wishing to bring Sacred Sexuality into their pastoral counseling, must be properly trained. And it takes a person of extreme integrity to hold this pathway or offer this counseling. Accountability and oversight will be part of the process to ensure all held in a container of safety.

What is Sacred Sex?

Sacred Sex is a channel with Divinity through which a healing occurs: sexual, emotional, and spiritual release using intentional touch, sensation, sensation play, energy, love, orgasm as sacred healing

What is a Sacred Sexual Service?

Some within CAW may practice Sacred Sexuality as part of their personal spiritual practice. In all interactions, Consent is essential. Sacred Sexual Service spans a wide spectrum of kink positive, freedom of expression, therapeutic healing, and sexual acts which may include some or all of the following.

Tantra
Sex Magick
Group Rituals
BDSM Kink
Platonic sensual Touch
Sacred Massage

16. Sacraments in the CAW

by Oberon Zell & Liza Gabriel
(from *CAW Membership Handbook,* 3rd Edition, 1997)

SACRAMENT IS SOMETHING REGARDED AS HOLY, OR SACRED. ordinary acts or substances may be elevated to the status of Sacraments in a ritual context, thereby becoming gateways into a greater awareness of the beauty and power of the BIG PICTURE and our part in it. Article II, Paragraph 16 of the CAW Bylaws lists as one of our Purposes: "To make provisions to establish and ordain various Sacraments of the Church of All Worlds." Such sacraments may grouped into three categories: Actions, Rituals and Substances. *It is absolutely prohibited in the CAW that anyone ever be compelled or coerced into partaking of any Sacrament without their full knowledge and consent.*

Actions

Sacred Sexuality— The appropriate expression of sexuality at each season of life is essential to a life fully lived. Sex is a source of power, creative as well as procreative. This power commonly derives from polarity, a charged attraction of opposites, but that is only one of the many ways that sexual energy flows. People of similar qualities or of the same sex generate pleasure and power together. The giving and receiving of sexual pleasure is an endlessly varied art.

We are born out of this act of pleasure. This miracle has been a source of awe and a method of magic from the dawn of time. We all have in us somewhere the naive and childlike belief that if sex can create us, sex can create anything. Out of such simple beliefs some of the most powerful and effective magic in human experience is woven. Our bodies are the particular piece of the Great Mother especially entrusted to us. In the experience of that sacred trust, Sex becomes an act of worship, engaging and awakening the God and Goddess in our partners. "For behold; all acts of Love and Pleasure are My rituals." (Doreen Valiente, "The Charge of the Goddess") Thus we sanction all loving and responsible sexual relationships between informed and mutually consenting adults, whatever their gender, number or practice. We also advocate safer sex practices.

Ritual Nudity— As in our founding novel, *Stranger in a Strange Land* (SISL), we encourage and practice (though we do **not** require!) "holy nakedness" in our Nests; and weather and privacy permitting, we conduct many of our outdoor rites "skyclad." Group skinny-dipping and hot-tubbing are long-standing traditions in the CAW. Naked bodies are honest, unpretentious, beautiful and sacred; we are "naked and unashamed!" We agree with "The Charge of the Goddess:" "And as a sign that you be truly free, you shall be naked in your rites." We support the establishment and maintenance of clothing-optional beaches, hot springs, and other sanctuaries for skyclad communion with Nature.

Environmental Action— As our prime deity is the Goddess of the Living Earth, we regard Her maintenance and protection as our most sacred duty. We are in strong alignment with the rallying slogan of Earth First!: "No compromise in defense of the Mother Earth!" We support all forms of non-violent environmental activism, including highway and park clean-up campaigns, tree plantings, and demonstrations against despoilers of Nature.

Magic— We define "Magick" as "the art of probability enhancement," or "coincidence control." The study, practice and mastery of such arts is a lifelong quest, involving the ability to formulate, embrace and shift the very paradigms that constitute our consensual "reality."

Rituals

Water Sharing— The communion ritual of Water-Sharing is the quintessential rite of the Church of All Worlds. The rite is conducted simply by offering a chalice of water to another, while saying such ritual phrases as: "I offer you water; may you never thirst;" "May you always drink deeply;" "Thou art God (or Goddess);" "Water shared is life shared."

We have affirmed that **Water-Brotherhood** may only be pledged in person, and face-to-face. We have learned that this sacred act is not to be entered into lightly or without careful thought; it is a lifetime commitment to a bonded relationship, in which water-sibs promise to always "be there" for each other. This is the deepest and most intimate form of Water-Sharing, held in the "innermost circle."

As for **group Water-Sharings,** we do not consider these to be pledges of water-brotherhood on the same intense level of commitment as the personal sharings, but rather a communion of acknowledgment. We recognize two levels of group Water-Sharing: the large "outer circle" sharing affirming kinship in the great "Circle of Life," wherein "water shared is life shared" with "all that groks," which, of course, "is God/dess;" and the "intermediate circle" sharing among those attending any Nest, coven, or small group ritual, affirming the bonds of the group.

Seasonal Celebrations— Central to all Pagan worship, including that in the CAW, is the annual cycle of seasonal "Sabbats" referred to as the "Wheel of the Year." Participating in these celebrations attunes us body, soul and tribe to the Great Round of Life's Mysteries: Birth, Growth, Death and Rebirth. The eight Sabbats are:

Ostara— Spring Equinox; Festival of Rebirth
Beltaine— May Day; Festival of Sacred Marriage
Litha— Summer Solstice; the Longest Day
Lughnasadh— First Harvest; Festival of First Fruits
Mabon— Autumn Equinox; Second Harvest; Festival of Harvest Home
Samhain— Hallowe'en; Final Harvest; Feast of the Blessed Dead
Yule— Winter Solstice; Festival of Returning Light
Oimelc/Imbolg— Festival of Waxing Light

Rites of Passage— These are rituals honoring and empowering life's significant transitions. Such passages include (but are not limited to) the following:

Being Born— rite of *seining,* or baby blessing, in which infants are presented to the community, given names, God & Goddess-parents, and blessing gifts;

Menarche/Puberty (attaining fertility)— ceremonies heralding girls' "first blood;" boys' coming of age;

Adulthood— rites declaring independence and legal responsibility;

Gender Reassignment— rites celebrating transition from natal gender to chosen gender identity;

Taking Mates— rite of *handfasting* (marriage);

Giving Birth— rites of delivery, motherhood and fatherhood;

Menopause (end of fertility)— rite of "croning" for women;

Elderhood— rite of "saging" for men;

Death— "last rites" include "passing," wakes, funerals and burials (or other disposition of the body, such as cremation and the scattering of ashes).

Initiatory Mysteries— An Initiation is a magical metamorphosis; a ritualized transformation experience that introduces one to a new level of reality. Initiations, meaning "new beginnings," may mark life transitions, as in Rites of Passage, or they may signify entry into a mystical society. CAW-sanctioned Mystery Initiations include those of various Traditions of Wicca and Shamanism, and the once-in-a-lifetime Eleusinian Mysteries.

Nest Meetings & Esbats— An "Esbat" is a full moon meeting of a Witches coven. Held in a ritual Circle, such gatherings focus on both worship and the working of magic—"probability enhancement"—for healing or other changes in the world. Nest Meetings of the CAW may be held as Esbats, New Moons, or more frequently as desired. The form is always a Circle, and Water is always shared in communion.

Personal Spiritual Practice— CAW Waterkin are encouraged to establish and maintain a daily spiritual practice. This may include setting up a household altar, offering prayers and *puja* (rites), morning and/or evening meditations or exercises, meal blessings, and such other routine rituals as seem appropriate to the individual.

Divination— There are many techniques of divination, or "far-seeing," all of which are honored in the CAW. These include (but are not limited to) the following:

Scrying— trance-gazing into a crystal, mirror, bowl of water, fire, etc.;

Tarot and other card reading— random selection, display and interpretation of archetypal symbols on painted cards;

Rune-casting— interpreting thrown stones inscribed with Norse or other runes;

The I Ching— ancient Chinese book of proverbs keyed to hexagrams;

Astrology— correlation of Earthly events with celestial patterns;

Augery— interpretation of synchronous natural events, such as the flight of birds.

Elements

Elements— The four Elements, **Earth, Water, Air,** and **Fire,** are actually the four states of matter: solid, liquid, gas and plasma, going from lesser to greater energy. These comprise the Body, Blood, Breath and Energy of Gaia. All of material existence is composed of these Elements in varying combination, and so we honor them in our rituals. Many also add **Spirit** as a fifth Element. Within these broad categories may be grouped all the Sacred Substances:

Earth

Primal Ooze— A delightful way to experience the conjoined Elements of Earth and Water is via "Primal Ooze." The latest scientific thinking has it that wet clay formed the original template for the formation of DNA, four billion years ago. A pit filled with smooth wet clay provides a truly wonderful mud bath for slippery hordes of Waterkin! Clay is also, of course, a wonderful artistic medium, and, when we add Fire, becomes the most enduring of all artifacts.

Cheez-Its— The first heresy declared by the Roman Catholic Church was the *Artotyrite* heresy; a practice of the Montanist sect, who ate cheese on their communion bread. In the Church of All Worlds we affirm the right to diversity in sacraments by honoring the Artotyrites with *Sunshine Cheez-Its* (accompanied with an explanation of the symbolism, jokes: "What a friend we have in Cheez-Its;" "Cheez-Its saves," etc.).

Of course, **Bread, Fruit,** or other foods (such as the special selection of "underworld foods" eaten in silence at the Samhain "Dumb Supper") may be shared "snack-ramentally" as well. All such foods are considered to be the body of the God and/or Goddess. The most common phrases to accompany the passing of food are: "May you never hunger," or "May you always have sufficiency."

Chocolate— Chocolate is widely recognized in Pagan Circles as the Fifth Element. Celebrants are known as "Chocolytes" though those who over-indulge are known as "Chocaholics."

Chocolate beverages were considered a drink for the Gods during the time of the Aztec Empire. In Tantric practices a couple would place a square of dark chocolate between their lips and eat to the middle where they would meet in a long passionate kiss. This not only raises the Kundalini (among other things) but evolves the use of the taste buds in oral satiation.

Chocolate has a divine taste that is orgasmic as it melts in your mouth. The theobromine causes a euphoric state which satisfies the deepest of desires and most compelling of cravings.

In circle, when sharing this "snack-rament," the most common phrases are: "Thou art sweet", "Thou art creamy," and for the darker time of year, "Thou art bitter sweet." When you have ingested this sacrament and reached true enlightenment, you achieve the realization that there "S'more than enough for everyone and some to share."
(—Aeona Silversong)

Water

Water— This is the prime "official" sacrament of the Church of All Worlds; read all about it in *Stranger in a Strange Land!* Water is the essential foundation of all Terrestrial life, comprising 80% of our body mass. Water is literally the very blood of the Mother; the chemical constituency of the blood in our veins is the same as that of the ancient seawater of four billion years ago, which we assimilated into our bodies as we developed in the oceanic womb of The Mother. We are all One— washed in the blood! Blood, sweat and tears are the waters of our lives. The physical properties of water, manifesting as solid, liquid and gas (Earth, Water and Air) at biologically compatible temperatures, and water's unique property of having a solid form that floats in the liquid, are what allows the possibility of life on Earth—and throughout the known universe.

Water-sharing by Nybor, 1997.

All CAW rituals include a Sharing of Water, from a simple communion acknowledging of our water-kinship with all Life, to the lifelong commitment of Water-Brotherhood.

Of course, other liquids, such as **Wine** or **Fruit Juice,** may be shared sacramentally as well; they all partake of the "essence" of Water. As we offer wine, we may say, "Wine shared is love shared;" with juice we often joke, "May you always be juicy!"

Coffee— The "Javacrucian Mysteries" of the Goddess Caffeina are enacted every morning in countless Pagan households and all Pagan events: facing the rising Sun and holding the Mug of Brewe, the celebrant takes a first sip, then elevates the cup and intones, "Gods, I needed that!" And means it. Then begins the daily recapitulation of ontogeny...

Sects of the Javacrucian Tradition vary mainly around additives to the Basic Brewe:

The Left Out Path
The Path of Delectable Darkness
The Milky Way
The Path of Sweetness and Light

Associated cults include Teaosophists, Rastacolians, Mateyanists, and Chocolytes.

Air

Breath— Breath is a rhythm which accompanies every moment. Unlike our heartbeats, we can consciously control breath; holding it, speeding it up, slowing it down, making it shallow or deep, raspy or smooth. Yet when we are asleep or unconscious, our breath continues. Because breath can be controlled both by the conscious and unconscious minds, it is used as a bridge between the two. In many languages the word for spirit and the word for breath are the same: *ruach* in Hebrew and *esprit* in French. In other traditions the word for breath and life energy are the same: *prana* in Sanskrit and *pneuma* in Greek. Breath has been used since prehistory not only as a bridge between the conscious and unconscious, but as a bridge between body and spirit. Breath is the foundation of most sacred sex practices. It is used in ritual to raise and focus energy and to bring an experience of full aliveness, embodying the spirit and inspiring the body.

Music— Music plays a central role in almost every religious tradition. Diverse groups of people can grow very close very fast through an experience of music or singing. Music fills the air around us embracing everyone present and echoing in our souls. The Pagan community in general and the Church of All Worlds in particular are blessed with many inspired musicians and bards and these folk contribute to virtually every Pagan ritual and occasion, often inviting everyone to join in. The two most ancient and widespread sacred instruments are voice and drum. Both are intimately connected to the rhythms of the body—the voice to breath and the drum to heartbeat.

Fire

Campfires— The most ancient and distinctively human experience is that of sitting around a campfire, sharing songs and stories with your clan. A campfire automatically forms the focus of a primal circle, and scrying into the flames may reveal many things... Firewalking also has been learned and practiced by some of us as an initiatory and transformative experience.

Annwfn Moon Circle by OZ.

Candle-Burning— Burning candles of selected colors may be used in spellwork. Some of the most popular color associations are:

    Red— Physical work, as in healing of people and animals; passion and sex;

    Orange— Pride and courage; heroism and attraction;

    Yellow— Mental work, meditation, etc.; intellect;

    Green— Vegetation, as in gardening; fertility and prosperity;

    Blue— Emotional work, love, etc.; peace and protection;

    Violet— Power, wealth and good fortune;

    Black— Blighting, binding and protection;

    White— Blessing, or anything you want!

Spirit

Psychedelics— Various plant-derived psychotropic chemicals have been used as sacraments in virtually every culture on the planet, including wine in Christian Churches and peyote in the Native American Church. These are "medicines" of great power, meant to be used only with reverence, and in a sacred manner. The magic of these sacraments lies in their ability to temporarily alter mundane consciousness and allow communion with the Gods. If such substances are to be used at all, it is the collective wisdom of the Ancient Elders that they should be used respectfully and reverently, with the full know-ledge and consent of the partaker.

From time to time, the CAW Board of Directors has legally registered resolutions to establish and ordain as sacraments, to be used in a sacred and ritualistic manner, with full reverence, various psychotropic herbs and substances which were not currently proscribed or designated as controlled substances by the laws of any known municipality, county, state, province or country. Two of these are: MDMA ("Ecstasy"), registered 4/5/85; and *Salvia Divinorum* ("Diviner's Mint"), registered 1/19/95. Such registration does not constitute a recommendation that these substances be partaken of, but rather an acknowledgment of their sacred nature.

Dance— One of the most primal and prevalent scenes in Pagan life is a fire circle with drummers and dancers. Both freeform dancing and circle dancing are essential parts of our rituals and celebrations. Expressing the joy, sorrow and beauty of our lives through our bodies and through dance affirms our identity as part of the natural world and prevents our rites from becoming mere head trips.

Humor— Pagans in general, and CAW Waterkin in particular, seem to have an inordinate fondness for humor and jokes, both clever and dumb. Puns especially are virtually a trademark of our sense of humor, and the references from which these are drawn are an affirmation of our common group heritage. Some of the most ubiquitous humor references in our tribe have included:

> **Monty Python** TV shows and movies;
> **Star Trek** TV series (all!) and movies;
> **Firesign Theatre** radio shows and albums;
> **The Addams Family** TV series and movies;
> **The Hitchhiker's Guide to the Galaxy** (by Douglas Adams) books, radio, TV shows, movies;
> **The Princess Bride** book and movie;
> **Pirate movies,** books, jokes, cartoons, etc.;
> **Science Fiction & Fantasy** (esp. Robert Heinlein, Roger Zelazny, Robert Asprin, Terry Pratchett...);
> **Filk Songs,** including endless verses to "Give Me That Old Time Religion!"

17. Rites of Passage

By Alder Moonoak & Oberon Zell
(from *CAW Membership Handbook,* 3rd Edition, 1997)

RITUALS OF TRANSITION AND LIFE CHANGES, CALLED "RITES OF Passage," mark significant periods in life, movement between life-stages, and personal transformations. These are rituals of honoring and empowerment. They are a public acknowledgment and recognition of growth. Just as the seasons pass in order, so do the stages of life. The inner and outer worlds mirror each other, so Rites of Passage provide a further link with the Earth and the Cosmos. Rites of Passage include coming of age, marriage or handfasting, pregnancy and birth, passage into Elderhood, handpartings, death and rebirth.

Birth

When a child is born it is a remarkable event; when a child who is loved by many and nurtured by a whole community is born, it is a miracle. When we gather to name and honor a new baby, we honor life itself. Other terms for this rite are *seining,* or baby blessing. At this time those who will nurture the child are identified: Goddessmothers, Godfathers, parents, siblings and other loved ones who may have a part in the baby's life are recognized before all. We pass the new baby around the Circle, with magickal gifts and blessings for long life, health and happiness: "Live long and prosper…"

Coming of Age

Centuries ago, this phrase originally meant "of age to marry," but in these days we no longer expect people to marry so young! Normally held between the ages of 11-13, the Coming of Age ceremony celebrates the onset of puberty in one's body and mind. From this point begins the exploration of our new and changing bodies. You must learn your own boundaries, likes and dislikes, and about your right to say yes or no when it comes to *your* body. Usually this rite is performed by adult members of the child's own sex, and may involve an initiatory ordeal and the giving of a magickal use-name.

Gender Reassignment

This can be as simple as having a menarche ceremony for a transwoman witchling when they start hormone therapy, or a ritual to celebrate a transman getting to experience puberty as a man. Some may want a ritual that ushers them from one gender to the other. The possibilities for inclusion are endless and effortless.

Adulthood

This rite can occur anytime between the ages of 16-21, depending on the individual and local laws concerning "legal maturity." This ceremony heralds the beginning of the journey into adulthood, adding adult attitudes, abilities, responsibilities and maturity to our best youthful attributes. The rite usually involves a sacred/special place, a "Vision Quest," and a "rebirth" into the community of adult men and women. Some symbol is gifted to the new adult and s/he is honored before all—often with a new magickal name.

Handfasting (Marriage)

Choosing to live with a mate or partner is a commitment to that person, a joining of two or more independent beings because they are *more* together than they are apart. Handfastings are made "for as long as love shall last" because even though a couple may stay together for the rest of their lives, they also may not, and both choices are honorable. This rite sends them off on a joint adventure, with as much joy and passion as possible! And if they should someday decide to part, a ceremony of **Handparting** will allow them to do so with honor and goodwill.

Parenthood

While Birth rites are centered on the baby, Parenthood is a ceremony for the new parents. It is a time for honoring the mother and father whose life journey has brought them to this place. We bless the new parents with a "baby shower" and a circle of love and support. This is a celebration, a party, a time for giving gifts, and of saying: "We're here if you need us—you don't have to raise this kid alone!"

Elderhood (Crones & Sages)

Elders, like children, are priceless treasures of our community. After the age of 50 or so, we may formally acknowledge and honor our Elderfolk for their wisdom, knowledge, skills, or whatever they have gained from their years on Earth. Often it's they who settle disputes, bless babies, and speak with greatest authority in councils. At this rite, another symbol may be gifted to them in recognition of their value.

Death/Rebirth

Death is a once-in-a-lifetime experience! Near or at the time of death, we give comfort and compassion in a **Rite of Passing.** Beloveds gather to say goodbye, and to send the spirit out through the Circle. We ask that they be blessed with peace, a time of rest, and then a new journey, a new birth. After death, we remember them with a gathering called a **Wake.** This is a farewell party where we share treasured memories and stories. A **Funeral** may follow, in which a few chosen speakers may deliver a *eulogy* ("good words")—speaking of the impact of the departed person's life on theirs, and on the world. Recurrent refrains are: "Let this memory lighten grief" and "What is remembered, lives."

A time of death is a sad time, but also one filled with hope and joy, for Death is part of Life, and just as the seasons turn, so we also will be reborn and continue. It is a time to let go and move on. Perhaps we may even have inherited a Guardian Angel in our lives: "May your spirit continue to guide us."

The Great Cycle, the Spiral leading ever forward, continues, one within the other: the moments of a day, the seasons of our lives, our lives themselves, generations, planets, stars, galaxies and universes, all turn in the great Circle of Life. One of which we are proud to be a part, because fun, adventure and growth are the greatest treasures I can imagine!

18. CAW Liturgical Structure

By Morning Glory and Oberon Zell

THIS IS A 13-STEP OUTLINE OF THE RITUAL STYLE AND ORDER OF Service generally used in the Church of All Worlds. It is offered here as a suggestion, but not a form to which you must adhere. One of the best things about Pagan rituals is that they offer so much room for creativity. This is the form taught in the Lifeways classes, and used as a starting point for creating more complex forms. It correlates with most standard ritual forms used throughout much of the Euro-American and Australian Neo-Pagan and Wiccan community.

I. BANISHING/CLEANSING
(optional; not used in all rituals)
   A. Smudging (with sage)
or: B. With words
   C. Asperging (with salt water)

I. GROUNDING
(optional; not used in all rituals)
   A. Guided meditation
    ('Tree of Life")
or: B. Physical movement

II. CASTING THE CIRCLE
*(Deosil/*clockwise for "doing;" *widdershins/*counterclockwise for "undoing." All movements within the ritual should follow direction of casting.)
   Walk circumference with a tool
    (blade, wand or crystal).
   A. Start in East for Deosil Circles
   B. Start in West for Widdershins
    Circles *(i.e. Samhain)*
or: B. All dance circumference
   C. Chanting/singing
   D. Visualization

IV. CALLING THE QUARTERS
   A. East (Air)
   B. South (Fire)
   C. West (Water)
   D. North (Earth)
Optional: E. The Great Above (or
    Spirit)
   F. Great Below (or Abyss)
   G. The Center (or Faerie)

V. INVOKING DEITIES & SPIRITS
   A. The Goddess
   B. The God
Optional: C. Ancestors
   D. Faerie
   E. Animal Totems
   F. Higher Self

VI. STATEMENT OF PURPOSE
Articulating and clarifying the purpose and intention of the ritual.

VII. THE WORKING
Conducting/enacting the actual rite—may be a ritual drama, spell-casting, healing. initiation, etc.

VIII. POWER RAISING & RELEASING
   A. Chanting and/or Drumming
   B. Dancing (circle or spiral)
or: C. Meditation
   D. Great Rite (sex) if appropriate

IX. COMMUNION
   A. Charging/Blessing and Sharing:
    1. Food (cakes, bread, fruit, etc.)
    2. Drink (water, wine, juice, etc.)

X. HIATUS
   A. Meditation
or: B. Discussion ("Sacred Bullshit")
   C. Sharing, announcements
   D. Business

XII. THANKS & DISMISSAL OF ELEMENTS & SPIRITS

  A. Deities/Spirits *(in reverse order of invocation)*
  B. Directions/Elements *(in reverse order of invocation)*

XIII. OPENING THE CIRCLE

(in reverse direction of casting) Done in same manner as it was cast, i.e. by song, dance, sword, hands, etc.

Notes: Maximum participation is elicited. Parts are shared among participants. There is usually personal ritual preparation before the rite begins.

This can include silent meditation, a purifying bath, fasting, jogging, dancing, stretching, etc.

Circles are usually cast *deosil*, starting in the East, or seasonal direction; but a Samhain the Circle and Quarters are cast and called *widdershins*, beginning in the West Greek rituals are also normally done Widdershins.

In the Southern Hemisphere the Directions, movements and seasons are reversed from those here indicated.

Sample Ritual Elements

CIRCLE CASTING *(Mike Fix)*
I cast the circle of ancient lore
Waves upon a timeless shore
With no beginning, nor an end
Always knowing foe from friend
Ouroboros, of legends old
Rings of power, forged in gold
Wheel of the year, circle of stones
Cycle of life, from birth to bones
A ring around the silv'ry Moon
I cast you now, o ancient rune!

INVOCATION OF GODDESS
(Ayisha)
Lady of the Earth, the Oceans and Wind
Mother of the Fire that bums within!

INVOCATION OF GOD *(Ayisha)*
Lord of the Dance, bringer of Light
Untamed God, give us delight!

POWER RAISING *(Starhawk)*
We are the power in everyone
We are the dance of the Moon and the Sun
We are the hope that never died
We are the turning of the tide!

FOOD BLESSING *(Moonrose)*
Holy Mother Earth,

Yours is the power
To grow, to destroy, to give birth.
We conjure You now
By seed and by shoot,
By flower and fruit,
By light and by love,
From below and above,
In Your ancient names:
Gaea, Hertha, Pachamama.
Grant us the blessings of Your body;
Thank you for the blessings of Your body!

QUARTER DISMISSALS
(Traditional)
0 mighty Guardians of the North,
[West, South, East]
We thank you for attending our rites.
Go if you must; stay if you will.
But ere you depart
To your fair and lovely realm,
We bid you hail and farewell!

CIRCLE OPENING *(Gwydion)*
All from air, into air
Let the misty curtains part
All is ended, all is done
What has been now must be gone
What is done by ancient art
Must merry meet and merry part
And merry meet again!

18. Suggestions for Conflict Resolution in CAW

by Anodea Judith and Oberon Zell

ERIODIC CONFLICT BETWEEN MEMBERS OF GROUPS OR ORGANIZA-
tions is unfortunately an inevitable risk of people working together in the creation of
something new. These conflicts can undermine the success of all that you may wish to
accomplish. Conflict can be poisonous. or it can be transformed into medicine.

In the Church of All Worlds, we do not necessarily advocate avoiding conflict at
all costs, remaining forever in the safe zones of expected behavior, but instead try to
see conflict as fruitful material for one's growth. This growth occurs through resolution
of the conflict, as it forces change. It is important that attempts at resolution occur in
as timely and respectful a way as possible.

The following guidelines are a distillation of various processes used by the CAW
community to resolve conflict. We offer them as resources to fall back upon when
conflict arises.

1. Avoid pouring gas on the flames. Conflicts are emotionally charged issues.
When we are involved in them, it is very tempting to discharge this energy by talking
to others. Often this takes the form of malicious gossip, exaggeration of issues. and
triangulated conversation. (Triangulation is talking to a third party about someone who
isn't there.) Containment provides the hermetic seal that allows alchemical
transformation. It requires discipline.

2. Write down your issues. If you feel you are not ready to talk to the person with
whom you have trouble, you can dissipate some of the charged energy by writing a
fictitious letter about how you feel. This letter would not be mailed or delivered but
exists for you to validate your own feelings, get your thoughts in order, and discharge
pent-up energy in a way that doesn't cause further harm.

In this private work-through of feelings, examine the patterns that may have
existed elsewhere in your life. What part did you play in creating this conflict? Does
this happen in other relationships? What are the particular triggers that are hardest for
you to deal with? What is it about those triggers that has the most potential for your
own growth? Learn to separate "what happened" from your *interpretation* of what
happened. For example, what happened was that no one called you to inform you about
the meeting. Your interpretation might be that "people are deliberately excluding me."
Interpretations are the foundation of difficult feelings and may be wrong. Look for
several different interpretations before drawing conclusions about someone else's
behavior.

3. Attempt to talk to the person in question. While this may seem utterly
obvious. it happens all too seldom. Don't assume the person can't hear your objections

until you have done the previous step and then attempted to communicate. You may be surprised. If the attempt fails, pay careful attention to where the communication breaks down. Things to try when communicating are:

A. Active listening. When the other person is speaking, listen closely, without judgment, and then repeat back to them what you think they said, whether or not you agree, whether or not it seems fair, accurate, or justified. This might take the form of "It sounds like you feel unappreciated and misunderstood." No editorializing!

Then ask the person to do the same for you. After you are both clear that what you have to say has been heard by the other person, then you can begin to talk about the differences in your viewpoints—still using the principle of active listening. "'So it sounds like you disagree with my statement that I do most of the housework and feel underappreciated when I say that."

Many problems result from misunderstandings, communication snafus, differing expectations, and over-commitments which can usually be resolved by clarifying things.

B. Use "I" statements and avoid "you" statements. "I" statements begin with the pronoun I; "you" statements with you. An "I" statement says, "I feel very misunderstood." A "You" statement says, "You never listen to anything I say." We can argue with accusations made of us, but we can't argue with how a person feels. "I" statements produce less resistance and antagonism.

C. Take a win-win approach. Try to avoid polarization of either/or, win/lose dynamics. Take the idea that a solution exists that will please both parties, and that otherwise, anyone's categorical win is by nature another's loss. Avoid having to be "right."

If attempts to communicate one on one are unsuccessful:

4. Restate the issues that need to be addressed, in writing.

5. Call for a mediation. We have devised several approaches towards resolving disputes. What follows is a Procedure for interpersonal Conflict Resolution, approved by the CAW Board of Directors, deriving from Celtic. African, and Native American tribal custom and the authors' personal experience in mediation and counseling. It is most useful in dealing with disputes between individuals:

Interpersonal Conflict Resolution Procedure

I.   **Conditions. ~**
   A.   <u>**Agreement to Conflict Resolution Procedure.**</u> *Membership in the Church of All Worlds implies an agreement to submit to a sanctioned procedure for Conflict Resolution.* Refusal to participate in a Conflict Resolution Procedure,

and especially, refusal to attend a Conflict Hearing in which one is charged of wrongdoing, could be considered grounds for revocation of membership and/or privileges of membership in the Church under CAW Bylaws Article 8—Paragraph 5.

B. **Parties.**
   1. **Plaintiff** is the party making a complaint, charges or accusations of wrongdoing. Most commonly the Plaintiff is the one who will initiate a call for a Conflict Resolution Procedure.
   2. **Accused** is the party charged with wrongdoing. Sometimes an Accused will seek to avoid a Conflict Resolution Procedure, particularly if the dispute is a serious manner, with serious charges. In other cases, one who feels unjustly accused may be eager for a Hearing, and may, in such a case, even be the one to initiate the Procedure.

II. Mediators, Advocates, Tribunal & Elders' Council.

   A. **Mediator.** If both parties are able to talk with each other then they select a mutually-agreeable and willing Mediator to help them resolve the dispute. The Mediator makes arrangements with both parties for an acceptable time and place to hold a Hearing, as well as appropriate compensation for their time and trouble. The Mediator makes sure that both parties have a copy of this Procedure and agree to follow it.

   B. **Advocates & Tribunal.** If the parties are not speaking to each other, then each party selects a willing Advocate, usually beginning with the Plaintiff, whose Advocate must then contact the Accused to select a Defense Advocate. The Advocates then select a mutually-agreeable and willing Mediator, thus creating a Tribunal. The Tribunal arranges with both parties for an acceptable time and place to hold a Hearing. as well as appropriate compensation for their lime and trouble.

   C. **Elders' Council.** The disputing parties and/or their selected Mediator(s) may decide and agree to bring the matter before an Elders' Council. Such a Council may be composed only of Elders in the CAW, or it may comprise Elders in the wider Pagan community, such as the Grey Council, depending on the scale of relevance of the dispute. The Council makes arrangements with both parties for an acceptable time and place to hold a Hearing. as well as appropriate compensation for their time and trouble. It may be that the party initiating the Conflict Resolution Procedure will appeal directly to the Elders' Council. or a dispute may be referred to the Elders' Council by some other body of the Church, such as the Clergy Council, the Board of Directors, or a Nest Council. In such cases the Elders' Council must see to it that both parties have acceptable Advocates and a Mediator, or that either or both parties agree to waive Advocacy and/or Mediation.

III. The Hearing.

   A. The Hearing may be open or closed, at the discretion of either of the disputing parties.

1. **<u>A Closed Hearing</u>** shall consist only of the disputing Parties, their Advocates, their Mediator (or Elders Council), and such Witnesses as either party wishes to bring forward. If either party wishes to present witnesses, this must be made known to the other party prior to the hearing. and with enough advance notice so that the other party may also present witnesses. If the parties are not on speaking terms, this communication shall be made by way of their Advocates.

2. **<u>Open Hearing</u>.** In addition to the above, either or both parties may invite other members of the community to attend and witness the proceedings, either by specific invitation, or by public announcement. If one of the parties intends to open the proceedings, the other party must be so informed prior to the Hearing. If the parties are not on speaking terms, this communication shall be made by way of their Advocates.

B. **The Mediator** (or Elder's Council) seeks a resolution based on **Truth** and **Justice.** The function of the Mediator is to balance the issues with as much fairness and objectivity as is humanly possible. It is important that the Mediator avoid judgments, condemnation, heady analysis, or biased support.

C. **<u>Procedure.</u>** The Mediator asks each party in turn: *"Let's hear your story."*

1. The first statement must be made by the one initiating the Procedure (for convenience here assumed to be the Plaintiff), who shall explain their case, charges and accusations as succinctly as possible. The Mediator must make sure that these three questions are addressed: *"What happened? Why did that happen? What happened as a result of that action?"* Upon conclusion of the Plaintiff's statement, the Accused's Advocate and/or the Media1or may ask questions for clarification.

2. The second statement must be made by the Accused, who shall explain their case as succinctly as possible. The Mediator must make sure that the same three questions are addressed: *"What happened? Why did that happen? What happened as a result of that action?"* Upon conclusion of the Accused's statement, the Plaintiff's Advocate and/or the Mediator may ask questions for clarification.

3. Witnesses for the Plaintiff, if any, may then be brought forward by the Plaintiff's Advocate, and shall present their accounts. They may then be cross-examined by the Advocate for the Accused and/or the Mediator.

4. Witnesses for the Accused. if any, may then be brought forward by the Accused's Advocate. and shall present their accounts. They may then be cross-examined by the Advocate for the Plaintiff and/or the Mediator.

5. Addressing each in turn, beginning with the Plaintiff, the Mediator asks: *"What would you need to redress the grievances you have? What would you be willing to give in order to redress the grievances you caused? How do you feel Justice would be served here? What do you think would be fair?"*

The Mediator must listen attentively to all sides and then make suggestions and offer assistance towards redressing the issue in a way that takes the needs and offerings of both sides into account. It is most important that both panics feel that Justice has been served. There may be situations, however, in which

Compassion may be a higher value than Justice... In any case, an agreement must be reached, even if it is an agreement to disagree, or to part company.

- a. Moving from an individual assessment to a systemic viewpoint can take the pressure off individuals and decrease polarization. In other words, seeing the conflict arising out of a greater field of oppression, be it the dysfunctions of the whole group, the pressures acting upon the people in question at the time, or even the influence of the larger society, helps to diffuse the blaming and shaming that interferes with being receptive to difficult communication.
- b. Sometimes a simple apology is sufficient to elicit forgiveness and healing. Since conflicts are seldom black-and-white, a mutual apology is ideal. A meaningful apology requires five steps:
    - i. **Acknowledgement** that a mistake was made and/or harm was done.
    - ii. **Repudiation** of the error or harm.
    - iii. **Apology.** (Forgiveness often follows.)
    - iv. **Commitment** to change ways or repair damage.
    - v. **Restitution:** "How can I make it up to you?"
- c. If the Accused refuses to acknowledge wrongdoing and apologize for it, the Plaintiff may choose, for their own healing, to forgive the Accused anyway.

6. When an agreement has been reached, it shall be written up by the Mediator or a designated Recorder, and presented to both parties to sign and elate. If the agreement includes restitution, or actions to be taken in the future, these shall be so noted.

7. If the parties in dispute cannot be brought to an agreement, then the Mediator and the Advocates shall consult among themselves to reach an agreeable resolution. If such a resolution cannot be reached among the Tribunal. then the matter shall be referred to an Elders' Council for a resolution or judgment decision.

IV. Enforcement.

- A. If one or both of the parties fails afterwards to abide by the agreement reached through this Procedure, the case shall be referred back to the original Mediator, who shall then turn to the local Nest Council, Elders' Council, Clergy Council, or Board of Directors (depending upon the Mediator's sense of which body should be addressing the issue). The appropriate governing body must then make a judgment decision.
- B. Penalties for failure or refusal to abide by an agreement reached through mediation may range through the following degrees:
    1. Banishment for a designated period from Church facilities or events.
    2. Suspension of Church privileges for a designated period.
    3. Revoking of Church membership.
    4. A legal restraining order placed against the offending party.
    5. Other legal recourse (i.e. a lawsuit).

19. Conflict Resolution in CAW

By Brahn th' Blessed (Samm Dickens)

CONFLICT IS NOT MISCONDUCT; IT IS BENEFICIAL TO HIGHLIGHT THIS point at the start of this chapter. Conflict is only an aggravated disagreement among people, maybe even close friends who are not normally expected to display such hostility. Misconduct, on the other hand, typically involves inappropriate and possibly even criminal behavior. The **Church of All Worlds** (CAW) has a policy paper available regarding misconduct, entitled "**CAW Code of Behavior.**" It recommends six positive steps toward exhibiting acceptable behavior.

- (1) Be Excellent to Each Other!
- (2) Be Excellent to Yourself!
- (3) Honor Diversity!
- (4) Take Personal Responsibility!
- (5) Consider the Consequences!
- (6) Walk Your Talk!

The **Code of Behavior** then delineates a longer and more detailed list of offensive actions, misbehaviors which *"will not be tolerated by CAW"*. These include:

Bullying and **harassment,** such as:
- Shaming
- Intimidation
- Physical or verbal threats of any kind
- Coercion of any person in any way (*this can be subtle at times and includes flattery and seduction, but the results are equally devastating*)
- Racial, religious, gender-based, sexual preference-based, ethnic, or any other kinds of slurs
- Brandishing a firearm or knife (*or any instrument that could be considered as a weapon*), or threatening anyone with bodily harm at CAW events
- Defacing, damaging or destroying property
- Fighting, or in any other way creating a disturbance which is disruptive or dangerous to others

Harassment includes, but is not limited to:
- Persistent verbal comments that reinforce social structures of domination [*related to gender, gender identity and expression, sexual orientation, disability, physical appearance, body size, race, age, or religion*].
- Deliberate intimidation, stalking, or following
- Harassing photography or recordings
- Sustained disruption of talks or other events
- Advocating for, or encouraging, any of the above behavior.

Sexual Misconduct includes, but is not limited to:
- Inappropriate physical contact
- Unwelcome sexual attention
- Intimidating with size or gender
- Stalking/following
- Constant "jokes" or innuendo
- Acting on the assumption of continuing consent (*just because there was consent once does not mean there is still consent*)
- Consistent pattern of Oversharing
- Taking pictures/recordings without consent (*especially if they could be used to shame/embarrass*)
- Manipulating/coercing to get sexual favors
- Any consistent pattern of harassment where one is made to feel physically unsafe because of the threat (stated or implied) of sexual violence.
- Advocating for, or encouraging, any of the above behaviors.

Finally, the CAW has a *"Misconduct Committee to investigate and make recommendations to the CAW Board of Directors (BoD) regarding any individuals causing harm within the CAW community or Church. Such harm includes, but is not limited to: sexual misconduct, harassment, bullying, coercion, severe breaches of ethics, or any behavior that impactfully inhibits the safety and health of the **Church of All Worlds**, its community and the people in it."*

If a conflict involves an accusation of wrong-doing, either misbehavior as described above or even a criminal act, the procedures of the **CAW Code of Behavior** shall take precedent AND a law enforcement agency shall be notified as necessary. If a conflict involves no actual wrong-doing, if it is only a disagreement, however hostile the proponents of opposing views have become, it can be resolved by communication, compromise, and compassion.

The Power of Ideas. Passion is welcomed in the CAW as it indicates a (sometimes fierce) conviction to an idea—a cause or a dream, a theory or a purpose, a personal goal or a group project. But passion can be misdirected; however certain we are in our conviction about some idea we cherish, that certainty does not necessarily correspond to infallible truth, and we are ill-served by passionate conviction to an unworthy idea. Nonetheless, we are seldom forced to recognize such errors; often we just lose our enthusiasm over time with our inability to share our passion with others. Consequently, we do not often confront our misjudgments, and do not realize fully how imperfect our human minds can be in committing to the various ideas that direct our lives. If we understood how often our actions are motivated by bad ideas, we might more humbly appreciate the dreamers who achieve their goals, and we might more carefully examine the ideas we hold dear before we commit to them.

Most interpersonal conflict is a conflict between conflicting ideas, so it is necessary that I discuss what I mean by "**ideas**". Our minds are loaded with hundreds of ideas of various kinds and powers. By *kind of idea* I mean that we may conceive an idea to be a thought, a concept, a notion or opinion, a word in any language, an article of faith, a theory or hypothesis, a simple conjecture, a supposition or assumption, a known fact, a deeply held religious conviction, a political viewpoint, propaganda, or any other fundamental or aggregate mental construct, however chronic or accute; kinds of ideas are myriad and general. They may be true or false, valid or invalid, positive or negative, all in varying degrees.

And ideas may be weak or mild, moderate and influential, or powerful and dominating. Martin Luther King's **Dream** was a very powerful idea of justice and equality in his life and in the lives of millions of other people, so powerful that it drove them to courageous and dangerous actions and sacrifice of their personal safety and security, even of their lives. At the bottom extreme, I have this notion: that my example of Dr. King and the civil rights movement was an effective example to illustrate the power of ideas. This notion is weak and insubstantial as ideas go; it may be accurate or not, it is a passing concern, but it illustrates the thousands of small ideas that contribute to larger ideas.

What you want for lunch is a small idea. *How you feel about a local political event* is a moderate idea. *Christianity, Islam, Hinduism, and all other such religious traditions* are massively powerful collections of ideas, although each of them is a single, massively aggregate idea as well. So I hope you get the idea about what all an idea can be and how powerfully motivational an influence it can exert in our lives. We all severely, and often disastrously, underestimate the influence of ideas in directing the course of human activity and history, and our personal lives and destinies.

The Heart is Master of Us All. I know one more very important thing about the ideas we have. I know that we don't get to believe just any ideas. There's a guardian at the gate of our minds. We have innate propensities to believe some ideas, and innate propensities to reject others. I'm a Pagan now, but I was a Christian as a child, raised by Christian family in a Christian world. Through all my teenage years, I was a Christian, but I encountered Pagan things in books and in nature. These encounters presented Pagan ideas that were easy for me to accept; my heart had ample room for Pagan ideas. At the same time, the ideas I read in my Bible did not all ring so true, did not all resonate with my inner self; I began internally to reject Christianity, piecemeal at first but in whole by the time I was a nineteen year old in the Air Force. After my service years, I never returned to the church. My heart—Don Juan Matus calls it my "innermost predilection"—lured me away from the Christian church and onto the Pagan path that I have followed ever since.

It is impossible to believe in an idea that your heart rejects or to reject an idea that your heart believes; no-one can make you believe an idea that your heart rejects, no-one can make you reject an idea that your heart cherishes. You can't do it, no-one else however ruthless can do it. The mind is not free to believe only for convenience, or to believe anything in the absence of sincere attachment; to try would only be pretense and folly.

Therefore when two ideas conflict, the two parties who hold those ideas also conflict, or at least tend to disagree. If the ideas are powerful, the conviction of the adherents will be passionate, the conflict will be heated, perhaps hostile. If one or more of the parties has an innately aggressive personality, the conflict can be greatly enhanced because conflict is not only engendered by ideas but by personalities as well.

Conflict Resolution in CAW

Step One: Talk it Out Between You. In the **Church of All Worlds** (CAW), we encourage people in conflict to understand each other better and thereby reduce the conflict and hostility. For some of us, reducing hostility and resolving conflict comes easily, while for others of us it is an arduous process that leaves a bitter taste. CAW recommends that conflicting parties, as a first step, *try to resolve the conflict among themselves*, using the basic principles of conflict resolution:

(1) **two-way communication** (*speak your truth and listen intently*),
(2) **respect for the other persons** or the other party (compassion),
(3) **acceptance** of *the rights of other people to hold ideas contrary to your own*, and
(4) a **willingness to compromise** where possible and *seek a point of consensus* between all parties concerned.

Step Two: Advocacy. If the conflict between the two parties is too severe and they are unable to come to terms, they should carry the resolution effort to the second step and each acquire an **advocate** who has no vested interest in the issue of contention and allow those advocates to seek a resolution to the conflict. Bear in mind that a conflict is NOT resolved if acrimony continues between the parties in conflict, even if the conflicting ideas are brought by compromise to a consensus synthesis. It is better that the parties achieve an end to hostilities and leave the conflicting ideas unresolved; that is, if they "agree to disagree".

Step Three: Arbitration. As a final (third) step in resolving the conflict, when the advocates are unable to help the adversaries to resolve all the anger, disrespect, and hostility between them, the adversarial parties and/or their advocates may select a neutral **arbiter** to make a judgment on those issues that obstruct resolution of the conflict and restoration of amicable relations between the parties. The advocates must present to the arbiter each and every issue that seems to prevent a full resolution; then the advocates must argue the point of view of the parties they represent (the parties may also testify as witnesses under the direction of their advocates); and finally, the arbiter, having heard all arguments regarding outstanding issues, shall take up to **one week** to produce an *arbitration decision* on each issue (each *article of arbitration*) presented.

Each party in the conflict must either consent or object to each article of arbitration in the decision, by initial/signature on the arbitration document. Consent is not agreement; it is only acceptance of the arbitration. Objection is refusal to accept the arbitration. The arbiter must then decide if further discussion of any objectionable articles is warranted in order to achieve full consensus and resolution of the conflict. The arbitration procedure is repeated for any and all objected articles.

If *all issues in the dispute are resolved* to the point of mutual consent and if both parties exhibit an end to hostilities and a restoration of amicability and mutual respect, the conflict is considered to be **resolved**. If a number of issues, but less than a third of those presented to the arbiter, remain unresolved, the conflict may be considered

partially resolved, as long as both parties are cordially agreeable to it. Else, the conflict is considered **unresolved** and outstanding.

If one or both parties are unable to overcome their hostilities even with arbitration, they may be **suspended from CAW** until they can show reasonable proof that they have put their negative feelings behind them; that decision would lie with the Board of Directors or with anyone they may appoint to direct conflict resolution for the church.

Conclusion and Summary. It is okay to get mad at a friend, to be mad at a friend, but not to stay mad at a friend. If you are angry with someone in the church, talk out your issues, speak your truth with calm sincerity. Passion for a cause is fine, but intemperance is not helpful. You cannot command respect when you are not showing respect, so listen intently to the truth spoken by your adversary; don't judge them, understand them. If you suppose that your adversary is wrong, then it must be clear that you may be wrong just as easily and may blindly believe you are right. Certainty after all is only an emotion. Your prolonged anger is wrong; subdue your anger and then cleanse it from your heart, for it is only a friction and an obstruction.

Sit with your adversary face to face, tear down any emotional walls you feel between you and build a bridge from your heart to theirs (*this meditation will help you communicate effectively*). Do not fear conflict; it is your ally. If you understand conflict, why it happens and how it can be domesticated for the mutual benefit of everyone, you can resolve conflict and grok yourself and your friends more deeply at the same time. This is the way of wisdom.

Brahn th' Blessed!
August 28th, 2022

Maypole dance at Annwfn. Beltane 2012. Photo by Richard Ely.

20. Tribal Conflict Resolution

By Jim Fish, 11/28/2001

THE PRINCIPLE IS "SAFE SPACE, SACRED SPACE." ALL MASKS ARE OFF. Honor this or begone. Thou art Beloved.

First, the telling of truth, fully, without agenda, before the witnesses. That's pretty basic. It's also pretty hard. This requires:

(2) the surrender of attachment to the point of view, the investment in being right in the matter, surrender to Spirit, and the willingness to be just naked in the face.

(3) "Do thy will" has a corollary, which is, "Actions always have consequences."

(4) In a conflict, you must realize that no matter how justified you feel you are, regardless of what may or may not have actually happened in your experience, the fact remains that the end result has been a that a Beloved feels that harm has been done.

(5) Would you rather be right, and remain stuck, or surrender this for the sake of enlightenment and an insight and a healing of the matter?

(6) The only way to do this is to come clean. First with yourself. What did you bring to the party?

(7) Remember that you are Cause in the Universe. The situation you are resisting has come about through your doing, to teach yourself something so profound that you needed all this drama to bring it to yourself as a wake-up call. A gift to yourself. Stop fighting it, and pay attention. How, why, and with whom did you create this drama?

(8) The purpose of the witnesses is to witness, as you unfold, not to "take sides" and add confusion to your process by adding negative energy.

(9) Perhaps forgiveness and restitution and vows are in order? This is not for us to say, but for you to realize and real-ize.

(10) Behind every seeming conflict there is a higher truth. When discovered, this truth proves to be worth the effort. Your life can be transformed by copping to it. We witnesses are here to cheer this when it shows up.

(11) Higher stakes. We are all committed here to the game of Insight. We look at what is going on, in the space of looking inside ourselves. What is the value? What can be learned? Where is the epiphany? What is the breakthrough? What is the lesson? We want to learn from you as you work out your knot, knowing that your work untangles our own.

(12) When all is said and done, all is forgiven.

So mote it be.

21. Consensus Decision-Making

By Liza Gabriel, 1999

IT HAS COME TO MY ATTENTION THAT ALTHOUGH OUR CAW Bylaws direct us to use consensus, we have limited information about what it is or how to use it. I recently attended "The Art of Community" conference, a three-day conference held by the Fellowship for Intentional Community. The people and communities I met who use consensus consider it a skill that requires training.

As many of you know, I am the coordinator of a small volunteer, nonprofit called The Body Sacred. I have been chosen, for three years in a row, by consensus. We have used consensus successfully in meetings of five to fifty people over the last six years. We have successfully handled a budget of about $15,000 per year and have functioned in the black throughout our six-year history. We did all this without having any intellectual agreement about what consensus is.

Here are some of my impressions so far about consensus:

Consensus is a 350-year old method of participatory decision making created by The Friends (The Quakers). The Quakers have written records of the successful use of consensus dating back to its inception. They use it in large and small groups to make decisions of all kinds; business, politics, religion, community matters etc.

In consensus as they practice it there is a trained moderator who stands outside the decision-making process. (This would apply to groups of more than seven or groups in which there was a difficult dispute.) This moderator has some qualities in common with the "fair witness" of SISL.

There are many unfavorable stories about consensus floating around and no doubt there is some learning to be had from these too. We often hear about consensus as some outmoded sixties thing that causes endless processing and burns everyone out. This impression began in Berkeley and other places in the sixties when secular political groups such as Students for a Democratic Society attempted to lift consensus out of its original spiritual context. These well-intentioned people did not have enough experience, nor did they take the time to educate their communities. This created a tradition of poorly trained, uninformed, inexperienced people using the term consensus for all kinds of chaotic and poorly functioning situations. Our church is to some degree a victim of that tradition.

Consensus is an effective tool that is currently being used well and wisely and in many variations by many progressive organizations both secular and Sacred. Its roots are much closer to our own values than the roots of other decision-making processes. That may be why the founders of our church felt its use was important. I have given Starwhite one of my tapes on consensus as a Yule Gift. In my next report, I hope to supply more information in the form of a brief resource guide. In the meantime, anyone interested can contact the Fellowship of Intentional Community. They have materials for sale on consensus and would be happy to point you to more. Their contact info is: phone/fax: 660 883 5545, email: fic@ic.org, website: www.ic.org. My friend CT Butler also wrote a fine book on consensus. I don't have his current contact info.

Looking back on my own intuitive practice of consensus so far, I can see times when I made mistakes. Not listening well enough is how I would sum them up. There are quite a few skilled trainers and consultants in consensus with decades of experience in creating positive, participatory atmospheres for decision making. I intend to seek training and guidance, and I invite others to join me. If there are others out there with training or experience in consensus, I welcome your input and suggestions.

Consensus can be used well and poorly and does not solve all problems by a long shot. What I love about it is that inherent in its structure is the desire to honor and integrate all viewpoints. As we know from the story of the fairy who was not invited to the party, all viewpoints have their influence whether we invite them to the table or not.

As a politician friend of mine is fond of saying, you can't legislate morality. No structure can substitute for good will and an energy of cooperation, communication, and community. That being said not all houses are equal. A sustainable structure is worth having. A good house is worth the care it requires.

Consensus Decision-Making

The decision-making process used by Quakers (aka Friends of Seekers of the Truth) is a simple, time-tested model that moves a group towards true consensus. The key aspects of Quaker process can be effectively applied in any consensus decision-making process:

- Begin and end with a few minutes of silent worship for grounding and centering.
- Sit in a circle
- Agree on the agenda and timeframe
- Discussion involves active listening and sharing of information, both facts and feelings.
- Norms limit number of times one asks to speak to ensure that each speaker is fully heard.
- Norms limit repetition and long speeches.
- Norms include a short silence after every comment so deliberations are truly thought-full.
- The clerk's (Quaker term for facilitator) role is to be a neutral 'shepherd' of the discussion. If the clerk wishes to offer a personal opinion, s/he explicitly steps out of the neutral role for a moment.
- The clerk identifies areas of agreement and names disagreements to push discussion deeper.
- Dissenters' perspectives are listened to and embraced.
- When the clerk feels the meeting is close to consensus, s/he will describe "the sense of the meeting" which is the clerk's estimate of the as-yet-unspoken consensus.
- When no one objects to this estimate, the group drafts a written minute of the sense of the meeting.
- The group as a whole is responsible for the decision, and the decision belongs to the group.
- The goal is "unity, not unanimity."
- Important decisions are often "seasoned" until the next meeting to ensure truth and unity.

Resources

Pagan Clergy Training Programs
by Oberon Zell, Primate

IN 1967, WHEN THE CHURCH OF WORLDS FIRST BECAME PUBLIC AS a "Pagan" church, there were no schools or programs available for training Pagan Clergy. Indeed, following Mr. Heinlein's prescription in SISL, I had to enroll in a small Christian seminary (Life Science College, in Rolling Meadows, IL) to receive my Doctor of Divinity degree, which qualified me for ordination in CAW on Dec. 21, 1967.

CAW received our Incorporation papers in Missouri on March 4, 1968. We immediately opened a temple on Gaslight Square, St Louis, with a coffee house in the basement, and began holding classes in Pagan Philosophy, as well as a book-study program we called the "Human values Course." We mapped out the criteria for a 9-Circle "Progressive Involvement Program" (PIP), which I began publishing in the first issues of *Green Egg* (starting March 21, 1968).

While the original vision of the 9-Circle PIP was a guide for self-actualization, it also became our training program for CAW Clergy, and attaining 7th Circle resulted automatically in ordination as a Priest or Priestess. This program was greatly refined and deepened as the RINGS (Requirements Invoking Network Growth System) during our 3rd phase (the "2nd Phoenix Incarnation"—1978-2002), backed up by Anodea Judith's "Lifeways" program. But for decades, CAW's was pretty much the only Pagan Clergy training program around (other than what training was offered in various Traditions of Witchcraft to attain degrees). So in order to qualify as a Priest or Priestess by our standards, advancement in the CAW RINGS was the only option.

However, in this current 4th Phase (the "3rd Phoenix Incarnation"—2005-), there are now a number of Pagan seminaries and Clergy training programs available. CAW's "Lifeways" and RINGS are no longer the only options, and we wish to encourage our people to explore whatever else may be available and appropriate for their own path and Calling. Therefore, we have uncoupled our program for Clergy training and ordination from the RINGS, and, while a CAW Priest or Priestess still must be at least 6th Circle, reaching 7th is no longer an automatic ordination. In this Incarnation of CAW, Waterkin of the 3rd Ring (Circles 7-9) are known as "Beacons."

So here is a list of currently-available Pagan seminaries, oviaries, and other programs for Clergy training. Any of these may meet the expected qualifications for ordination, and be so listed on our Clergy Application. Other studies and experience particularly relevant for CAW Clergy would include:

1. **Theatre** (all aspects: acting, directing, scripting, staging, makeup, costumes, sets, props);
2. **Counseling** and psychotherapy (including hypnotherapy, mediation, and conflict resolution);
3. **Divination** (particularly Tarot, but other systems may also be useful);
4. **Service** (house cleansings, banishings, shieldings, bindings, rites of passage, spellwork, healings, exorcisms, handfastigs, funerals, public action…);
5. **Ritual** (see *Creating Circles & Ceremonies*).

Ardantane http://Ardantane.org

Ardantane is an independent, registered 501(c)(3) non-profit corporation established in 1996 in the state of New Mexico. Founded by Azrael and Amber K, Ardantane is a Pagan learning center and seminary. They have a small physical campus of several buildings on 25 acres, with limited overnight lodging facilities on site and in the nearby town of Jemez Springs. Ardantane's core curriculum areas include Healing Arts, Pagan Leadership, Magic and Witchcraft, Shamanic Studies, Pagan Spirituality, and Sacred Living. 11 faculty members are supplemented by various guest speakers. Most classes are held over a weekend at the Ardantane campus. 38 classes are listed in their catalog.

Cherry Hill Seminary http://CherryHillSeminary.org

Located in Columbia, SC, Cherry Hill Seminary is a privately-owned Pagan seminary program based on the Communitarian philosophy of the sacredness of connections and community building. Founded in 2001 by Macha Nightmare, Patrick McCollum, and Don Frew, the Seminary currently offers training for ordination in two primary areas: Public Ministry and Pagan Pastoral Counseling. Its programs are offered primarily online. 16 faculty members are listed. Students pay a basic admissions fee, and are also required to join the Communitarian Church for an additional fee.

Grey School of Wizardry http://www.GreySchool.com

Founded and incorporated by Oberon Zell in 2004, based on his *Grimoire for the Apprentice Wizard*. Received 501(c)(3) as an educational and charitable organization on Sept. 27, 2007. Physical cam-pus in Whitehall, NY. Virtual campus on 2nd Life. Current Headmaster (as of 2022) is Nicholas Kingsley. More than 500 online classes in 16 Departments for Majors and Minors, taught interactively by a faculty of qualified practicing experts. GSW is a secular school, not affiliated with any religion, but many classes are relevant to Pagan Clergy—especially in the Depts. of Nature, Healing, Divination, Lifeways, Ceremony, and Lore. 7 levels; Journeyman Letter issued upon graduation. Youths (11-18), Adults (degree program), and Magisters (non-degree, access to all classes). Residential programs are now available at Highspire campus in Whitehall.

Hoodoo Rootwork Correspondence Course

http://www.hoodoo@luckymojo.com

Created in 2003 by Cat Yronwode of the Lucky Mojo Curio Co. in Forestville, CA, this is a comprehensive course in Hoodoo herb and root magic. 52 weekly lessons are all online and in the hardcover textbook, *Hoodoo Rootwork Correspondence Course*. An important supplemental reference book is Cat's *Hoodoo Herb & Root Magic*. The other major reference is Cat's online book, *Hoodoo in Theory & Practice*, which is available free to students. Students are invited to join an online community where lessons and assignments are discussed and questions answered by Cat. Satisfactory completion of the 8 homework assignments earns a Certificate of Completion.

Order of Bards, Ovates & Druids (OBOD) http://www.Druidry.org

The Order of Bards Ovates and Druids, founded by Ross Nichols, began to offer a distance-learning course in Druidism in 1988 and since then over ten thousand people from all over the world have taken the first year's course, which is followed by an optional two further levels of study. The course includes membership in the Order and is divided into three stages or grades that correspond to the three traditional divisions of the ancient Druids: those of the Bards, Ovates and Druids. Each grade has its own initiation. Initial registration fee with a monthly fee to receive mailed packets. Each package contains four lessons to study (in audio or text format or both), and a copy of *Touchstone* – a monthly magazine.

Sacred Mist College www.workingwitches.com

Founded by Lady Raven Moonshadow in 1996 and brought online in 2002, Sacred Mist College offers training leading to Ordination as a Wiccan High Priest or Priestess. The Sacred Mists Tradition is based on Celtic Traditional and Faerie Wicca, with the College teaching a broad introduction to other Wiccan Traditions with an Eclectic flair. Trained and experienced personal mentors provide assistance with lessons. Tuition includes access to interactive and in-depth extension classes, which include subjects such as Tarot, Potion Craft, Candle Making and Magick, Kitchen Witchcraft, Healthy Witches, Scrying, Pendulum Use, Runes, Palmistry, Reiki, Ogham, Astrology, Numerology and many others. A Certificate of Degree Attainment is emailed upon completion of each Degree. Initial registration plus a monthly tuition fee.

Woolston-Steen Theological Seminary http://WiccanSeminary.EDU

Established in 1999 by the Aquarian Tabernacle Church, WSTS offers a choice of three campuses: one virtual (Second Life) and two physical campuses in Atlanta, GA, and Seattle, WA. Weekly online classes and monthly symposiums are held on both U.S. coasts. 11 faculty members teach Associate, Bachelor, Masters and Doctorate programs of over 40 varied courses, in 8 levels. Tuition is $80 per course, or students may participate in a membership program for full access, on an income-based sliding scale. In 2000, WSTS was authorized by the Washington State Higher Education Coordinating Board to issue degrees in Pagan ministry, the first in the nation.

Essential Books for Pagan Clergy

Adler, Margot, *Drawing Down the Moon: Witches, Druids, Goddess-Worshippers, & Other Pagans in America Today.* 1979; expanded 3rd edition Penguin, 2006.

Bonewits, P.E.I., *Real Magick: An Introductory Treatise on the Basic Principles of Yellow Magic.* 1971; revised edition Red Wheel/Weiser, 1989.

Brock, Janice & MacLer, Veronica, *Seasonal Dance.* Samuel Weiser, 1993.

Chappell, Helen, *The Waxing Moon: A Gentle Guide to Magic.* Links, 1974.

Cunningham, Scott, *Wicca: A Guide for the Solitary Practitioner.* Llewellyn, 1989.

Cusack, Carole H., *Invented Religions: Imagination, Fiction & Faith.* Ashgate, 2010.

Eilers, Dana, *The Practical Pagan: Common Sense Guidelines for Modern Practitioners.* New Page Books, 2002.

Hardin, Jesse Wolf, *Gaia Eros.* New Page Books, 2004.

Harrow, Judy, *Wicca Covens: How to Start and Organize Your Own.* Citadel, 2000.

Haugk, Kenneth C., *Antagonists in the Church.* Augsburg Books, 1988.

Heinlein, Robert, *Stranger in a Strange Land*, Ballantine, 1961 edition.

Hoffer, Eric, *The True Believer: Thoughts on the Nature of Mass Movements.* 1951. Harper Perennial Modern Classics, 2010.

Jaynes, Julian, *The Origin of Consciousness in the Breakdown of the Bicameral Mind.* Houghton Mifflin Co., 1976.

Kirsch, Jonathan, *God Against the Gods: The History of the War Between Monotheism and Polytheism.* Viking Adult, 2005.

Moonoak, Alder, *Radiant Circles: Ecospirituality and the Church of All Worlds.* John Hunt Publishing, 2010; 2022.

Nema, *The Priesthood: Parameters and Responsibilities.* Black Moon Publishing, 1995.

Pratchett, Terry, *Small Gods,* 1992; Harper reprint, 1993.

Shlain, Leonard, *The Alphabet vs The Goddess.* Viking Adult, 1998.

Slater, Herman (Ed), *A Book of Pagan Rituals.* Samuel Weiser, 1978.

Starhawk, *The Spiral Dance: A Rebirth of the Ancient Religion of the Goddess.* 1976; 20th Anniversary Edition, HarperOne, 1999.

Sulak, John & Vale, V, *Modern Pagans,* Re/Search Books, 2001.

Von Forslun, Tamara, *Pagan and Witch Elders of the World: Past and Present.* Xlibris Au, 2020.

Wood, Robin, *When, Why…If: An Ethics Workbook.* Livingtree Books, 1996.

Zell, Oberon & the Grey Council, *Grimoire for the Apprentice Wizard.* New Page Books, 2004.

________, with the Faculty of the Grey School of Wizardry, *Companion for the Apprentice Wizard.* New Page Books, 2006.

________, **& Morning Glory, *Creating Circles & Ceremonies: Rituals for All Seasons & Reasons.*** New Page Books, 2006.

________, ***GaeaGenesis: Conception & Birth of the Living Earth.*** Left Hand Press, 2022.

Appendix 1:
Primates' Statement
on Communication Courtesy

Oberon Zell & Alder Moonoak, Nov. 21, 2010

THERE'S NO QUESTION THAT POSITIVE AND EFFECTIVE COMMUNI-cation can be challenging for most of us. As *homo sapiens,* we've been speaking for millions of years and writing for thousands, so you'd think it would get easier with practice; yet we still regularly converse in ways that don't accurately get across to others what we're thinking or feeling. Relationships of all kinds provide us with endless opportunities to mis-communicate and to be misunderstood. Add to this the toneless and detached qualities of the Internet and you have a recipe for frequent communication problems.

The members of a religious community are in an active relationship with each other, so all the challenges of maintaining 'right speech' apply, except with added import, since churches generally purport to live spiritual lives that bring to bear moral and ethical beliefs onto the character and tenor of their interactions. They usually seek to serve as good examples to others and have a special responsibility to do so to the best of their ability.

In the case of our Church, this commitment to interacting in a 'spiritual' manner—that is, imbued with the highest and deepest qualities of compassion, respect, and love reflecting the divine—takes on even more gravity because we have a history of poor communication that has resulted in real divisions and ill-will within our organization. Such collapses in positive feelings and (inter)connections have occasionally resulted in the loss of otherwise committed and wonderful members who were discouraged by these patterns of inter-church conflicts.

For these reasons, and because the health and well-being of the Church is the responsibility of all members—and particularly of the Primate—this statement on communication courtesy is being created:

> In all communications with each other, members of CAW are to conduct themselves in their wording and tone with the utmost courtesy and respect, bringing to bear on their interactions an ambiance of politeness, kindness, and tolerance—conversing and discussing rather than arguing, seeking cooperation and consensus rather than conflict, and in general behaving in the spirit of the Church's deepest values and practices.

We're not saying it's an easy task, only that it's worthwhile. For those who, for various understandable reasons, don't accept or cannot manifest these guidelines, some accommodation which doesn't involve regular communication within core Church discussions will be sought, if so desired. For those who, for inexplicable reasons, continue hostile, argumentative, rude, or combative speech patterns, another, perhaps more appropriate, church will be recommended.

Appendix 2:
CAW Clergy Successions

Year	Date	#	Born	Priesthood	Ministers
2022	8/29	42	5/9/70		Terry W. Hughes
2022	8/26	41	3/18/74		Tanya M. Chiles
2022	5/22	40	6/15/53		Terry Brussel-Rogers
2019	11/22	39	2/4/81		Luis Valadez
2019	11/1	38	2/19/59		Dianna Morningstar
2019	2/16	40	3/6/66	Terrie Wolfe-Lee	
2019	2/16	39	2/8/79	Wynter Weiss	
2018	7/8	37	4/22/58		Samina Pitrello
2018	5/1	38	5/19/80	Jonna Towel	
2018	5/1	36	3/8/78		Susan "Seasons" Price
2018	5/1	35	12/21/75		Ryan Towel
2018	5/1	34	5/1/70		Bradley Lee
2018	5/1	33	3/6/66		Terrie Wolfe-Lee
2018	2/1	32	11/26/73		Bryan Altaker
2017	12/21	31	4/14/50		Harlan "Moonstorm" White
2017	11/19	30	1/12/69		Shady Blackfish (Matthew Rick)
2017	10/5	29	8/27/82		Edward Fish
2017	5/1	28	5/19/80		Jonna Weidaw
2017	3/21	37	10/18/67	Peter Brabyn (Australia)	
2017	3/13	27	11/24/42		Charlyn Scheffelman
2016	11/5	26	12/4/80		Meia Joy Yumi
2016	11/5	25	8/28/52		Judith "Mama Maureen" Barnett
2016	10/31	36	3/18/60	Alder Moonoak (died 10/12/2022)	
2016	10/31	35	1/22/47	Jacqueline Omi Mackenzie (Ecuador)	
2016	10/13	24	6/19/69		Cara Lynn Vecsera
2015	8/1	23			Jeremiah Waterchilde
2015	8/1	22	7/27/73		Sherry Froman
2015	8/1	21	9/2/69		Scott Sumers
2015	8/1	20	10/23/55		Janet Christian
2015	7/9	19	6/3/58		Rebecca Crystal
2014	11/9	34	6/19/76	Tim Emert	
2014	10/5	18	2/17/69		Tom Mozzetti
2014	10/5	17	12/31/74		Michelle Boyle
2014	10/5	16	2/12/88		Daisy Night
2014	10/5	33	7/4/57	Francesca Gentille	
2013	9/15	15	1/29/83		Elizabeth Bradford
2013	9/15	14	6/1/62		Dawn Davidson
2013	9/15	13	9/21/82		Catherine Murphy
2013	9/15	12	8/30/74		Sophia Amelia

Year	Date	#	Born	Priesthood	Ministers
2013	9/15	11	7/4/57		Francesca Gentille
2013	9/15	10	6/19/76		Tim Emert
2013	4/24	32	2/21/44	Willowoak Istarwood (died 7/8/2020)	
2012	1/15	31		Margaret Fyer (Australia)	
2012	1/15	30		Kerrieann Winkley (Australia) (retired)	
2012	1/15	29	1/15/43	Martha Babineau (Australia)	
2011	12/21	9	4/28/56		Ken Wills (Australia)
2009	12/22	8	3/15/57		Julie Epona O'Ryan

Third Phoenix Resurrection – International (above this line) (2005-present)

Year	Date	#	Born	Priesthood	Ministers
2002	8/9	28	1951	Kyril Oakwind (died 3/9/2013)	
2002	5/4	7	9/30/1917		Candy DeTray (died 2/8/2006)
2001	2/3	27		Anthorr Nomchong (Australia) (revoked)	
2000	2/12	26	3/26/52	Jack Ingersoll (retired)	
2000	2/12	25		Kris Jensen (died 11/21/2014)	
1999	12/22	6			Jim Looman (died 10/3/2004)
1999	11/1	24	5/23/71	LaSara Firefox	
1999	11/1	23	6/8/37	Marylyn MotherBear Scott	
1998	7/24	22		Ronn "Walks With Fire" Koester (resigned; died)	
1997	5/5	21	8/12/35	Farida Ka'iwalani Fox (retired)	
1996	11/7	20	2/22/60	Night Freedom An'Fey (resigned)	
1996	8/3	5	3/18/60		Alder Moonoak (died 10/12/2022)
1996	5/5	19		Maerian "Sun" Morris (retired)	
1996	3/24	4	6/25/38		Starwhite Lewis (died 1/6/2002)
1994	12/21	18	4/11/40	Richard Ely (retired)	
1994	11/7	17	5/19/53	Avilynn Pwyll (resigned)	
1994	5/23	16		Fiona Judge (Australia) (resigned)	
1993	9/25	15		Aeona Silversong (retired)	
1992	8/21	3	2/21/44		Willowoak Istarwood (d. 7/8/2020)
1990	9/9	14		Deborah Hamouris (resigned)	
1985	5/1	13	12/1/52	Anodea Judith (retired as "Emeritus")	
1979	6/21	12		Orion Stormcrow Morris (retired)	
1978	9/21	2	11/30/12		Charlie Leach (died @2000)
1978	9/21	1	5/21/46		Gwydion Pendderwen (died 11/9/1982)

Second Phoenix Resurrection – Ukiah, CA (above this line) 1978-2002

Year	Date	#	Born	Priesthood	Ministers
1974	8/1	11	5/27/48	Morning Glory Zell (died 5/13/2014)	
1973	8/1	10	7/20/38	Donald Wildgrube (died 4/8/2024)	
1973	6/23	9		Roberta "Bobbie" Kennedy (inactive)	
1973	5/1	8	1/25/40	Carolyn Clark (died 9/1/2021)	
1971	6/21	7		Michael Hurley (retired)	
1971	5/1	6		Toni Kristin (inactive)	
1971	5/1	5		Ravi Kristin (inactive)	

Year	Date	#	Born	Priesthood	Ministers
1970	2/1	4	11/19/47	John Patrick "Tiny" McClimans (died 11/10/1996)	
1969	5/1	3	10/9/46	Tom Williams	
1968	3/21	2	4/7/44	Lance Christie (died 10/28/2010)	
1967	12/21	1	11/30/42	Tim Zell	

First Phoenix Resurrection (CAW) – St Louis, MO (above this line) 1967-1978)

Year	Date	#	Born	Priesthood	Ministers
1962	4/7	1	4/7/44	Lance Christie (died 10/28/2010)	
1962	4/7	1	11/30/42	Tim Zell	

Founding Phase (ATL) – Fulton, MO (above this line) 1962-1965)
(many Atlan watersibs – see Atlan Logbook)

Wheel of the Year by Katlyn Breen

Appendix 3.
Comparative Religion

By Oberon Zell
(adapted from *Handbook for Our future Parents*, 2024)

RELIGION IS A TRICKSY SUBJECT TO WRITE ABOUT. IN COUNTRIES dominated by the monotheistic faiths (Christianity, Islam, Judaism) most people grow up in families and communities that either practice some particular religion, or (generally in rebellion) none at all. Either way, the dominant paradigm is that of *monotheism*—One God; One True Right and Only Way (all others are false and thus evil). Even declared atheists disbelieve in the same singular God that the devout worship!

There are an estimated 10,000 distinct religions worldwide,[1] though nearly all of them have regionally based, relatively small followings. Four religions—Christianity, Islam, Hinduism and Buddhism—account for over 77% of the world's population, and 92% of the world either follows one of those four religions or identifies as nonreligious, meaning that the remaining 9,000+ faiths account for only 8% of the population combined. The "religiously unaffiliated" demographic includes those who do not identify with any particular religion, atheists and agnostics, although many in that demographic still hold various religious beliefs.[2]

Some churches (specifically fundamentalists and evangelicals) are fanatically adamant about compelling their children to accept their particular religious dogma, and punish them severely if they dare to question it in any way. Their primary values are obedience, blind faith, and believing what they are told to believe—regardless of whether it makes any sense. Such religions should properly be considered *cults,* with all the negative connotations of that term. They commonly foster abuse—verbal, psychological, physical and even sexual. And after having dogma forced down their throats from infancy, it is very difficult for children to grow up with any inclination or ability for critical thinking. Hence they fall easy prey to cultists and demagogues.

Therefore it is essential that responsible Pagan parents do not attempt to force any religion or dogma down childish throats. But that does not mean avoiding the subject entirely. Introduce your children to various religions in your neighborhood. Make the rounds of local church services and Sunday schools, and discuss with your kids the different perspectives of these. Attend interfaith events as well as Pagan festivals—take your children along—and get to know the respective clergy on a personal basis of mutual respect (if they are willing—which many will be). Of course, I hope you will also introduce your children to Paganism, which, as you're reading this, I presume you embrace. But if you don't, they'll probably find it on their own…

---

[1] African Studies Association; University of Michigan (2005). *History in Africa.* Vol. 32. p. 119.

[2] "Religiously Unaffiliated." The Global Religious Landscape. Pew Research Center: Religion & Public Life. 18 Dec. 2012.

Today, owing to their experience with the aforesaid abusive churches and cults, many people are so turned off by the very concept of religion that they reject it entirely, proclaiming themselves to be "spiritual" rather than "religious." People confuse religion with "Churchianity."

I think this is a sad thing. Spirituality is a personal matter—one's own relation with the sacred, the Divine. It has to do with a personal practice, prayers, devotions, small rituals… But *religion* is what we do in community with others of like mind and heart. And we need that! Religion does not have to be dogmatic or abusive—nor should it be.

The word *religion* literally means "re-linking" or "re-connecting." *Religiō* (Latin) is derived from *religare*: *re* ("again") + *ligare* ("bind" or "connect"). Julius Caesar used *religiō* to mean "obligation of an oath" when discussing captured soldiers making an oath to their captors.[3] Roman naturalist Pliny the Elder used the term *religiō* to describe the apparent respect given by elephants to the night sky.[4] Cicero used *religiō* as being related to *cultum deorum* (worship of the gods).[5]

A religion is a body of sacred myths, metaphors, observances and practices in a cultural context, which are designed to connect (re-connect) humanity with Divinity and heal the rift between dichotomized aspects of existence. We observe that the great dilemma and tragic *anomie*[6] of present-day human society seems at its root to be the alienation caused by splitting apart humanity and Nature, matter and Spirit, light and dark, man and woman, good and evil, Heaven and Earth. Religions are supposed to heal that rift. How are they doing?

Comparison of Major Religions

Here's a rough general comparison of the major religions of the world—Christianity, Islam, Hinduism, Buddhism and Judaism:

Christianity[7]

The Christian faith centers on beliefs regarding the birth, life, death and resurrection of Jesus Christ. There are more than 200 Christian denominations in the US and a staggering 45,000 globally, with a total of 2.5 billion adherents. These comprise 31.6% of the

---

[3] Caesar, Julius (2007). *"Civil Wars–Book 1." The Works of Julius Caesar: Parallel English and Latin.* Translated by McDevitte, W.A.; Bohn, W.S. Forgotten Books. pp. 377-378.

[4] Pliny the Elder. "Elephants; Their Capacity." *The Natural History, Book VIII.* Tufts University.

[5] Cicero, *De natura deorum.* Book II, Section 8.

[6] The concept of *anomie* in sociology can be defined as a state of normlessness, disorder, or confusion in a society when the standard norms and values are weak or unclear. This lack of social or ethical standards can lead to disconnection, deviance, and social instability among individuals. French sociologist Emile Durkheim introduced it and later expanded it by others like Robert K. Merton. www.simplypsychology.org/anomie.html. Accessed 2/28/2024.

[7] Editors, History.com, "Christianity," Updated 8/3/2021; Original: 10/14/2017. www.history.com/topics/religion/christianity

world's population, in two main divisions, Catholic and Protestant, which range from the benign (Unity, Quakers, Unitarian-Universalists…) to the malignant (Orthodox, Evangelicals, Dominionists, Roman Catholics, cults…). There are also outliers such as Amish, Mormons and Christian Scientists. Each of them considers all the others to be heresies, and the history of Christianity is bloodstained with brutal efforts to exterminate the competition. But they all pretty much agree on the following:

Origin: Founding Prophet, Jesus (Yeshua) of Nazareth (4 BCE-29 CE), believed to be the Son of God and "The Messiah." Following of 12 Apostles. Three years of preaching terminated by execution by crucifixion for blasphemy and sedition. Primary proponent, Paul/Saul of Tarsus (5-65 CE), who coined the terms "Christ, "Christians" and "Christianity."

History: Founded in Jerusalem upon crucifixion of Jesus in 29 CE. Established in Rome by Peter and spread by Paul throughout the Roman Empire. Dispersed after Romans destroyed Jerusalem in 70. Emperor Constantine lifted the ban on Christianity with the Edict of Milan (313). In 380, Roman Emperor Theodosius I declared Catholicism the state religion of the Empire, with the Bishop of Rome (the Pope), as the head of the Roman Catholic Church. In 1054, the "Great Schism" split Christianity into Eastern Orthodox and Roman Catholic churches. Crusades to capture Jerusalem (1095-1254). "The Burning Times" (1227-1736) killed hundreds of thousands. Martin Luther initiated the Protestant Reformation in Germany (1517).

Theology: Monotheism: a solitary male Deity, called "God"—creator and ruler of the cosmos. Also his son, Jesus, and "the Holy Spirit" (the Trinity); and in Catholicism, Jesus' mother, Mary, and an array of ascended Saints—along with a vast host of Heavenly Angels and Infernal Demons. The antagonist, or anti-God, Satan, also plays a powerful role. Christians believe God sent his only son, Jesus, as the *Messiah,* to save the world. They believe Jesus was crucified on a cross as a sacrifice for the forgiveness of sins and was resurrected three days after his death before ascending to heaven. Christians believe that Jesus will return to Earth in the "Second Coming" to rule the world for 1,000 years.

Some of the main themes that Jesus taught include: love God; love your neighbor as yourself; love your enemies and forgive those who have wronged you; repent of your sins; do as you would be done by (the Golden Rule); don't be hypocritical; don't judge others; be compassionate; help the less fortunate; you are God; the Kingdom of Heaven is within you.

Sacred Scripture: *Holy Bible. Old Testament* (Jewish), 39 books. *New Testament* (Christian), 27 books, of which the earliest written were the letters of Paul. The first four books—*Matthew, Mark, Luke* and *John*—are known as the *Gospels* ("good news"). Composed sometime between 70-100 CE, these provide accounts of the life and death of Jesus. A final book is *Revelations*—bizarre visions of the end of the world.

Special Practice: Communion—sharing of bread and wine, symbolizing Christ's body and blood, shed in sacrifice to redeem humanity.

Purpose: Personal salvation from "original sin" (disobedience of the mythical progenitors Adam and Eve in eating the forbidden fruit of the Tree of Knowledge of Good & Evil in the Garden of Eden).

Afterlife: Those who believe in Jesus and are favored by God's grace are "saved," and go to eternal bliss in Heaven; everyone else is consigned to suffer eternal torment in Hell. Catholics have an interim realm called *Limbo* where they await Judgement Day.

Islam[8]

The word *Islam* means "submission" (to the will of God). Numbering more than two billion, Muslims comprise 25.8% of the world's population, and make up a majority in 49 countries—particularly in the Middle East, Africa and Indonesia. Islam is the world's fastest growing major religion, projected to be the world's largest by the end of this century, due to the relative young age and high fertility rate of Muslims. Islam is divided into two main branches, *Sunnis* (85-90%) and *Shias* (10-15%). A third tiny branch is called *Ibadism* (~0.08%). There is bitter rivalry among them, and bloody efforts to exterminate each other, as well as rival religions, such as Hindus, Jews and Christians. But they agree on the following:

Origin: Founding Prophet, Mohammed (570-632 CE), Arabia.

History: In 610 CE Muhammad retreated to a <u>cave</u> near Mecca, where he received the first revelation of the *Quran* from the angel Gabriel. In 622, Muhammad performed the *Hijra* ("emigration") to Medina where he established his authority. By the time he died in 632 (at age 62) Muhammed had united the tribes of Arabia into a single religious polity. However, after his death, bitter wars of succession raged for centuries, continuing to this day. From the 8th-13th centuries, the Islamic Golden Age was a period of scientific, economic and cultural flourishing far surpassing Europe, which was in its Dark Ages.

Theology: Monotheism (a solitary male Deity, called "<u>Allāh</u>"—creator and ruler of the cosmos). Angels were created to worship God and also to serve in other specific duties such as communicating revelations from God, recording every person's actions, and taking a person's soul at the time of death. Also Shaitan—the Moslem version of Satan, the Temptor.

Sacred Scripture: The *Quran,* considered to be the verbatim word of God and the unaltered, final revelation. Muslims also believe in previous revelations, such as the *Tawrat* (the Torah), the *Zabur* (Psalms), and the *Injil* (Gospel). Abraham, Moses and Jesus are considered prophets.

Purpose: Islam teaches that everything in the universe was brought into being by God's command, and that the purpose of existence is to worship God.

Special Practices: Muslims must pray five times a day, facing Mecca. A pilgrimage to the *Kaaba* (a black meteorite in Mecca), called the "*ḥajj*" is to be done at least once a lifetime by every Muslim with the means to do so during the month of Dhu al-Hijjah. Genital mutilation on girls.

Afterlife: There will be a "Final Judgment" wherein the righteous will be rewarded in a heavenly paradise (*jannah*) and the unrighteous will be eternally punished in hell (*jahannam*).

---

[8] Editors, History.com, "Islam," Updated 10/23/2023; original 1/5/2018.
  www.history.com/topics/religion/islam

Hinduism[9]

Hinduism is the world's oldest recognized religion, with roots and customs dating back more than 4,000 years. 94% of the world's Hindus live in India. With 1.2 billion adherents, Hindus comprise 15.1% of the world's population. There are four major sects of Hinduism: *Shaivism, Vaishnava, Shaktism* and *Smarta,* as well as many smaller sects.

Origin: Unlike other religions, Hinduism has no single founder but is instead a fusion of various beliefs over centuries.

History: Around 1500 BCE, the Indo-Aryan people migrated to the Indus Valley, and their language and culture blended with that of the local indigenous people. The "Vedic Period," when the Vedas were composed, lasted from about 1500-500 BCE. The Epic, Puranic and Classic Periods took place between 500 BCE-500 CE. The Hindu Medieval Period lasted from about 500-1500 CE.

Theology: Polytheistic, with hundreds of Gods and Goddesses under a primary Trinity of *Brahma* (Creator), *Vishnu* (Preserver) and *Shiva* (Destroyer). Other important deities include *Devi*—the goddess who fights to restore dharma; *Krishna*—god of compassion and love; *Lakshmi*—goddess of wealth and purity; *Saraswati*—goddess of learning; *Kali*—goddess of time; *Ganesha*—elephant god who overcomes obstacles.

Sacred Scripture: *Vedas* (composed c. 1500 BCE). These are the *Rig Veda, Samaveda, Yajurveda* and *Atharvaveda.* The *Upanishads,* the *Bhagavad Gita,* 18 *Puranas, Ramayana* and *Mahabharata* are also considered important texts in Hinduism.

Purpose: All living creatures have a soul *(atman),* and all are emanations of the supreme cosmic soul of Brahma. Hindus strive to follow the *dharma,* a code of living emphasizing good conduct and morality. The goal is to achieve *moksha,* or salvation, which ends the cycle of rebirths to become part of the absolute soul.

Special Practices: *Puja* (worship). The giving of offerings, such as flowers or oils, to a god or goddess. Many annual festivals. Also, many Hindus make pilgrimages to temples and other sacred sites in India.

Afterlife: Hindus believe in the doctrines of *samsara* (the continuous cycle of life, death, and reincarnation) and *karma* (the universal law of cause and effect).

Buddhism[10]

Buddhism ("enlightenment") was founded more than 2,500 years ago in India. With an estimated 500 million to one billion followers, Buddhists comprise 6.6% of the world's population. Buddhism has historically been most prominent in East and Southeast Asia, but its influence is growing throughout the West. Today, many forms of Buddhism exist around the world. These include:

---

[9] Editors, History.com, "Hinduism," Updated 1/16/2023; original 10/6/2017.
   www.history.com/topics/religion/hinduism
[10] Editors, History.com, "Buddhism," Updated 9/5/2023; Original: 10/12/ 2017.
   www.history.com/topics/religion/buddhism

Theravada (Thailand, Sri Lanka, Cambodia, Laos, Burma); *Mahayana* (China, Japan, Taiwan, Korea, Singapore, Vietnam); *Tibetan* (Tibet, Nepal, Mongolia, Bhutan, Russia, northern India); *Zen* ("meditation"); *Nirvana* ("blowing out").

Origin: Founder, Siddhārtha Gautama (the Buddha—"Enlightened One"). (563-483 BCE), born in Nepal.

History: Born as a prince into a wealthy family, Gautama was moved by seeing suffering in the world. After six years of seeking, he found enlightenment while meditating under a Bodhi tree. He spent the rest of his life teaching others how to achieve this spiritual state. After Gautama died his teachings developed into Buddhism. In the 3rd century BCE, the Mauryan Indian emperor Ashoka the Great made Buddhism the state religion of India. Over the next few centuries, the thoughts and philosophies of Buddhists spread widely and became diverse.

Theology: As a non-theistic faith with no deity to worship, Buddhism is often described as a philosophy or moral code rather than an organized religion.

Sacred Scripture: The Buddha's most essential teachings (*dharma*) are known as "The Four Noble Truths." These are: The truth of suffering (*dukkha*); The truth of the cause of suffering (*samudaya*); The truth of the end of suffering (*nirhodha*); The truth of the Eightfold Path that frees us from suffering (*magga*).

Some of the most important sacred texts are: *Tipitaka,* thought to be the earliest collection of Buddhist writings. *Sutras:* There are more than 2,000 sutras, which are sacred teachings embraced mainly by Mahayana Buddhists. *Book of the Dead:* This Tibetan text describes the stages of death in detail.

Purpose: Followers of Buddhism focus on achieving "enlightenment"—a state of inner peace and wisdom. Upon reaching this spiritual echelon they attain *nirvana.* The ultimate goal is to no longer reincarnate.

Special Practices: Followers of Buddhism can worship in temples or in their own homes. Buddhist monks, or *bhikkhus,* follow a strict code of conduct, which includes celibacy. *Vesak* is an annual festival commemorating Buddha's birth, enlightenment and death.

Afterlife: As in Hinduism, Buddhists embrace the concepts of karma (the law of cause and effect) and reincarnation (the continuous cycle of rebirth).

Judaism[11]

Jews comprise 0.2% of the world's population, about 14 million people. Their influence is far greater than these numbers would suggest, however, as Judaism is the original Abrahamic parent religion of both Christianity and Islam. Most Jews today live in the US and Israel. There are several sects in Judaism, which include: ***Orthodox Judaism,*** a diverse sect that includes several subgroups, including ***Hasidic Jews.*** There is also ***Reform Judaism, Conservative, Reconstructionist*** and ***Humanistic Judaism.***

Origin: According to the Torah, God first revealed himself to a Hebrew man named Abraham who became the founder of Judaism.

---

[11] Editors, History.com, "Judaism," Updated 8/11/2023; Original: 1/5/2018.
  www.history.com/topics/religion/judaism

History: According to the Torah, in 1628 BCE, more than 1,000 years after Abraham, the prophet Moses led the Israelites out of Egypt (the *Exodus*) where they had been enslaved for centuries. God revealed his laws, the Ten Commandments, to Moses at Mt. Sinai. 40 years later, they invaded Palestine, setting up a Jewish kingdom. Around 1000 BCE King David ruled the Jewish people. His son Solomon built the first holy Temple in Jerusalem, which became the central place of worship for Jews. The kingdom fell apart in 931 BCE and the Jewish people split into two groups: Israel in the North and Judah in the South. In 587 BCE the Babylonians destroyed the first Temple and sent many Jews into exile. A second Temple was built in about 516 BCE but was later destroyed by the Romans in 70 CE, scattering the Jewish people in the *Diaspora* ("scattering"). Throughout history, Jewish people have been persecuted for their religious beliefs. In 1948, in compensation for the Holocaust, Israel officially became an independent Jewish nation by edict of the United Nations.

Theology: Monotheism. Jews believe in one God, named *Yahweh,* who revealed himself through ancient prophets, including Abraham, Isaac, Jacob, Moses, Solomon and others. Jews believe that their God made a special covenant with Abraham and that he and his descendants were chosen people who would create a great nation. Most Jews believe that their Messiah hasn't yet come—but will one day.

Sacred Scripture: The Jewish sacred text is called the *Tanakh* or the "Hebrew Bible." It includes the same books as the Old Testament in the Christian Bible, but they're arranged in a slightly different order. Around 200 CE, scholars compiled the *Mishnah*—a text that describes and explains the Jewish code of law that was previously orally communicated.

Purpose: Observing the Laws; obedience to Jahweh. Maintaining Jewish identity.

Special Practices: Circumcision of all males. No graven images or representational art. Worship in religious centers known as synagogues. Leaders are called *rabbis* ("teachers"). Celebration of several important days and events in history: ***Passover, Rosh Hashanah, Yom Kippur, High Holy Days, Hanukkah, Purim.*** From sunset on Friday until sunset on Saturday, *Shabbat* is observed as a day of rest and prayer for Jews, with special ceremonies.

Afterlife: No official dogma. Many believe the soul continues to the afterlife and receives judgment. Some anticipate a resurrection in the Messianic Age—a time known as the "world to come."

Minor Religions

Confucians/Chinese traditional religionists
comprise 394 million people—5.6% of the world's population.

Confucianism is a system of thought and behavior variously described as a tradition, philosophy, religion, theory of government, or way of life. Confucianism developed from teachings of the philosopher Confucius (551-479 BCE), during a time referred to as the "Hundred Schools of Thought." The *Analects* are a collection of his sayings.

Taoism is variously characterized as both a philosophy and a religion. Taoism emphasizes living in harmony with the *Tao*—the impersonal, enigmatic process of

transformation ultimately underlying reality. Despite the popularity of its great classics the *I Ching* and the *Tao Te Ching*, the practice of Taoism has not spread widely. Nonetheless, Taoist ideas and symbols such as *taijitu* have become popular throughout the world through *tai chi, qigong,* and various martial arts.

Sikhism is a monotheistic and panentheistic religion: There exists only one God, who is simultaneously within and all-encompassing. Sikhs comprise 26 million people—0.3% of the world's population. The Sikh homeland is the Punjab state, in India, where Sikhs make up approximately 58% of the population. Sikhs have emigrated to countries all over the world—especially to English-speaking and East Asian nations. Sikhism is also the fastest growing religion in Australia and New Zealand.
The basis of Sikhism lies in the teachings of Guru Nanak (1469-1539) and his successors. Sikh ethics emphasize the congruence between spiritual development and everyday moral conduct: *"Truth is the highest virtue, but higher still is truthful living."*

Jainism is an ancient Indian religion that traces its spiritual ideas and history through the succession of 24 *tirthankaras* (supreme preachers of *Dharma)*, with the first believed to have lived millions of years ago, to the 24th *tirthankara* Mahgavira, around 600 BCE. The three main pillars of Jainism are *ahiṃsā* (non-violence), *anekāntavāda* (non-absolutism), and *aparigraha* (asceticism). The function of souls is to help one another. Jainism has around 4.5 million followers (0.05% of the world's population), who reside  mostly in India. Outside India, some of the largest Jain communities are in Canada, Europe, and the USA. Japan is also home to a fast-growing community of converts.

Shinto is Japan's indigenous Nature religion, with 4 million adherents—0.05% of the world's population. There is no founder or central authority, with much diversity of belief and practice. Polytheistic and animistic, Shinto revolves around supernatural entities called the *kami*, which are believed to inhabit all things, including forces of Nature and prominent landscape locations. *Kami* veneration has been traced back to Japan's Yayoi period, 300 BCE-300 CE.

Zoroastrianism is an Iranian religion based on the teachings of the Iranian prophet *Zoroaster,* also known as *Zarathustra.* About 1000 BCE he founded a monotheistic religion with a dualistic  cosmology, predicting the ultimate triumph of good over evil. Zoroastrians worship a supreme benevolent deity of wisdom, *Ahura Mazda;* opposed to Ahura Mazda is *Angra Mainyu,* the adversary of all things good. The world's current Zoroastrian population is estimated at 110,000-120,000 people, with the majority residing in India, Iran, and North America; their numbers are thought to be declining.

Paganism

Rarely considered in religious surveys, modern Paganism is a revival and reconstruction of ancient Nature religions adapted for the modern world. It is a religion of the living Earth—a theological motif especially appropriate to the Aquarian Age, as Christianity was the dominant religion of the Piscean Age.

The most universal conception of deity among all Pagans—modern and ancient—is Mother Earth/Mother Nature: *Gaea, Hertha, Terra, Akna, Prithvi, Hòutŭ, Papa, Danu, Ninhursag, Pachamama...* Modern Pagans view humanity as a functional organ within the greater organism of all Life, rather than as something special created separate and "above" the rest of the natural world. Pagans seek not to conquer Nature, but to harmonize and integrate with Her. Paganism should be regarded as "Green Religion," just as we have "Green Politics" and "Green Technology."

The word "Pagan" derives from the Latin *paganus,* meaning peasant or country dweller. A term of derision among Christians, it has long been used by anthropologists to designate the indigenous folk religions of particular regions and peoples,[12] and by classical scholars to refer to the great ancient pre-Christian civilizations of the Mediterranean area (as in the phrase, "Pagan splendor," often used in reference to Classical Greece).[13] Indeed, the term is commonly applied to all polytheistic non-Abrahamic religions. Paganism is the ancestral religion of all humanity.

---

[12] "**Paganism: Gods of Nature.** In earlier times, before the true character of African traditional beliefs was understood, these people were called simply 'heathens.' They were poor benighted savages who 'bowed down to wood and stone.' The more accurate term today is 'pagans,' from the Latin *paganus,* a word which originally meant a peasant or countryman." ~"Africa," by James Wellard, *Man, Myth & Magic,* 1974; Part 1.

[13] The term "Classical Greece" refers to the period between the Persian Wars at the beginning of the 5th century BCE and the death of Alexander the Great in 323 BCE. … Besides the Parthenon and Greek tragedy, Classical Greece brought us the historian Herodotus, the physician Hippokrates and the philosopher Socrates. It also brought us the political reforms that are ancient Greece's most enduring contribution to the modern world: the system known as *demokratia,* or "rule by the people." ~"Classical Greece" by History.com Editors, *History.com.*

Modern Pagans include people identifying as Witches, Druids, Heathens, Celts, Hellenes, Khemetics, Baltics, American Indians, Hindus, Africans, Ifa, Shamans, Vodun, Rus, Polynesians, CAW Waterkin, Christo-Pagans, Judeo-Pagans, Buddheo-Pagans, Atheo-Pagans, and countless other cultural and ethnic Traditions.

The basic commitment of modern Paganism is to the re-integration or re-linking of people with ourselves, our fellow humans, and with the whole of living Nature around us. Pagans create no artificial demarcation between the sacred and the secular. To a Pagan, religion is ultimately a whole way of life, not some acts performed once a week in an authorized ritual. In this sense, Paganism *is* religion; the foundation, ground and source of all we may term "religious" *and* "spiritual.

The liturgical cycle of Paganism revolves around the Wheel of the Year. Rather than commemorating historical events, or the births and deaths of prophets and saints, Pagans throughout the world are united in celebrating the seasons of the natural year: Solstices, Equinoxes, and the cross-quarters between them. Many also celebrate the phases of the moon.

Paganism is re-emerging today because natural religion is a spontaneous evocation of the spirit of Life and will inevitably find expression in human cultures. The practices of the ancient Pagans occurred during a different era in culture, when we lived closer to the land and were more directly connected with farming and hunting.

Much of what was practiced in those days has been lost, due to millennia of persecutions, from the onset of the Iron Age, through the Inquisition and Witch-burnings, to the present day. Therefore, we cannot accurately say we practice ancient Paganism, but forms we are "remembering and inventing" together. The general structure of Neo-Paganism, however, is so varied as to be impossible to dictate to any large number of people. As the saying goes, ask two Pagans a question and get three different answers!

The Church of All Worlds

Founded in 1962 and incorporated in 1968, the Pagan Church of All Worlds may be the first religion to draw as much of its inspiration from the future as from the past, embracing science fiction as mythology with the same enthusiasm as we embrace the classical myths of ancient times. CAW "Waterkin" are future-oriented, meaning we care more about how we evolve and change than about how we got here and how we will come to an end. We embrace evolution, and in regarding the planet as a living organism, we embrace the evolutionary changes of the planet by bringing human consciousness into direct contact with the growing web of planetary consciousness through such structures as the global Internet.

Unlike many other religions, the Church of All Worlds is not focused on nostalgia for a Paradise Lost; we are actively involved in helping to save the present world as well as working to actualize a visionary future—seeding the Children of Gaea throughout the universe. With roots deep in the Earth and branches reaching towards the stars, we evoke and create myths not of a Golden Age long past, but of one yet to come...

Appendix 4:
Legal requirements
for Churches & Clergy

By Rona Coomer-Russell, Secretary
Our Freedom Pagan list

IN MY STATE OF TENNESSEE, ONE DOES NOT NEED AN IRS TAX 501 number to be considered a church. (this is stated clearly in TN Code 36-3-301, which discusses "ministers, preachers, pastors, priests, rabbis" or "other spiritual leaders who must be ordained or otherwise designated in conformity with the customs of a church, temple or other religious group or organization and such customs must provide for such ordination or designation by a considered, deliberate and responsible act" and have the "care of souls".) Thus, folks who get a Universal Life Church ministerial certificate over the web can indeed be ministers in Tennessee without any other proof. Other states are not this relaxed and require ministers to register, showing proof of either a) articles of incorporation or b) tax ID status AND a letter of good standing within that organization.

Regardless of IRS tax exempt status, all ministers who make over about $100 a year must file for "self employment tax."

In Tennessee, 501 is considered a benefit, but not a necessity. Ministers must pay self-employment tax, and churches who do not have 501 simply pay sales tax on all of their purchases. IRS 501 info at: http://ftp.fedworld.gov/pub/irs-pdf/p557.pdf

Spiritual Qualifications are listed on page 21, and there are only two: 1) that the religious beliefs of the organization are truly and sincerely held; and 2) that the practices and rituals associated with the organization's religious belief or creed are not illegal or contrary to clearly-defined public policy. The very next paragraph goes on to say that although churches need not file form 1023 to be exempt from federal tax, the organization may find it advantageous to do so. The other qualifications required are listed as well—mostly Articles of Incorporation, etc...

Page 15 also states that some organizations are already exempt without need to file.

If a church has gross receipts of less than $5,000, then that is one factor. The other is if they already meet the qualifications listed on page 21 prior to filing for 501.

So as you can see, it is best to find out what the state regulations are. If this person qualifies according to the state, then he may already qualify as a church with the Federal Government. The easiest way to find out if they are indeed considered a church with your state is to go down to the county clerk's office and ask. There are also archives of individual state laws on the web as well.

Appendix 5:
Clergy Confidentiality

By Elaine Porterfield

Pastor can't be forced to testify, state court rules

Friday, May 7, 1999
By Elaine Porterfield
SEATTLE POST-INTELLIGENCER REPORTER

A state Supreme Court ruling yesterday that a Tacoma pastor cannot be forced to testify about an alleged murder protects the sanctity of the confessional, supporters said yesterday.

The high court unanimously dismissed a Pierce County Superior Court's contempt charge against the Rev. Rich, ruling that he was protected by a state law that guarantees the confidentiality of religious confessions.

Prosecutors said the ruling significantly broadened legal protections to any religion, regardless of whether a religion has a recognized right of confession.

Theologians were buoyed by the decision. "This (ruling) will be the latest authority on the subject in the country," said Steve McFarland, director of the Virginia-based Christian Legal Society. "It will be hopefully a beacon light to warn other prosecutors away from this unconstitutional sandbar."

Hamlin, the ordained minister of the 75-member Evangelical Reformed Church in South Tacoma, was ecstatic. "I'm just thrilled that the state Supreme has ruled and ruled decisively," he said.

Last summer, the state Court of Appeals sided with Hamlin in a 3-0 vote, ruling the law protects clergy members if they believe they are hearing a confession out of a religious obligation. The high court's affirms the Appeals Court.

But the Supreme Court ruling does come with a caveat: The privilege enjoyed by a pastor who hears a confession could be nullified if there is a third party present -- that could affect the case at hand.

The case revolves around the death two years ago of 3-month-old Devyn Martin. County prosecutors charged Devyn's father, Scott Anthony Martin, with second-degree murder, saying he shook his son to death in a fit of frustration.

To try him, they said they needed to call Hamlin as a witness. They believe Martin confessed the slaying to Hamlin, who met with Martin three times after the baby died.

But Hamlin refused to testify, claiming that to do so would violate the privacy protecting what a penitent tells him in confidence. Pierce County Superior Court Judge Brian Tollefson found him in contempt.

Martin has been in custody since he was charged in 1997; his bail was set at $250,000. His trial was put on hold while the high court reviewed Hamlin's testimony.

Pierce County Prosecutor John Ladenburg said state law before ruling only protected confessions between a penitent and clergy in a religion with a recognized right of confession, such as the Roman Catholic or Episcopal churches.

"The other thing they (state justices) did, is very significant, is say that it's up to the priest to decide if it's a confession, as opposed to another that is non-confessional in nature," he said.

Ladenburg noted, however, that the high court also said that having a third party during the confession could negate the priest-penitent privilege.

In Martin's case, his mother was present as least during part of his conversations with Hamlin, Ladenburg said. The mother has told authorities she doesn't remember what she heard Hamlin and her son discuss.

Prosecutors also believe that yet another person was present when the pastor spoke with Martin a third time.

"We have evidence that at least two of the three times someone else was present during the conversations," Ladenburg said. "We'll give whatever we have to the judge and say, 'What do you want to do now?'"

Steven O'Ban, Hamlin's attorney, said a hearing will be held shortly for a judge to explore that question.

"As far as what will happen at the evidentiary hearing, I'm not in a position to guess," O'Ban said. "But I am confident the judge will not force Pastor Hamlin to testify."

Randy Maddox, a theology professor at Seattle Pacific University, said the court's ruling affirms an important religious right that dates to the earliest days of the church.

"If parishioners did not have the confidence (his confession) would remain confidential, it would remove an important tool of spiritual life," Maddox. "The promise that whatever is revealed remains private . . . goes back very far in the Christian tradition."

Said the Christian Legal Society: "The court has protected the sanctity of the confessional. You can confide in your clergy with the assurance what you say will stay between you and God. Troubled people can unburden their consciences to clergy without worrying their pastor will become the government's snitch."

Appendix 6:
Fees for Clergy Services

Oberon Zell (Church of All Worlds)

In my experience, $100 seems to be a typical honorarium for performing a handfasting, whether a fee or donation. That's in addition to feeding the officiating Clergy (there's usually a reception banquet following the ceremony), covering travel expenses, and putting them up overnight if need be. Here's what some other Pagan Clergy say…

Rev. Diana Paxson (The Fellowship of the Spiral Path; Covenant of the Goddess; The Troth)

I don't ask for money, but if the wedding is for a stranger, I'll accept a donation. If I've had to put in extra time to write a new ritual for them, or spent money on transportation or supplies, I take the money, otherwise I pass it on to the Spiral treasury. People usually offer around $100 for a wedding.

Rev. Jacqueline Mackenzie (Aquarian Tabernacle Church; Church of All Worlds – Ecuador)

I think we should ALWAYS take care of that none of us work for less than $100 a simple service OR $18-$20 an hour in the USA – including being paid for all writing, planning, transportation, etc.

The MOST I have been paid for Clergy Services outside CAW or ATC was $125 for about 3 days before and after a wedding. I did three separate funeral services for the same (wealthy) man and was given nothing.

Rev. Ellen Evert Hopman (Druid: Ár nDraíocht Féin; Keltria)

I only did one wedding. Charged $150 for the day.

Rev. Paul Beyerl (The Rowan Tree Church, The Tradition of Lothloriën)

The only service for which we consider a fee appropriate is the Handfasting. Typically the 'basic' fee is $75. With the exception of a house blessing, the other ritual services do not take much time beyond the actual ritual, other than a 15-20 minute phone call with scheduling and planning.

A Handfasting has variables. Oftentimes the work beforehand can be a couple of hours. The amount of set-up is usually much more involved. A Handfasting either takes place in our space which means preparation to accommodate all of the guests and usually a feast/reception. If it is off-site then we have driving time. And there is usually the expectation that we will be there for the reception.

There is an expectation that there will be a donation to our church (not money directly to Clergy) and sometimes there is nothing as we leave it up to the couple. If I am asked for a figure, the variables include now far away the venue is, how much time is involved, whether they want just me; but most of the time they want me and my partner (who is also Clergy). Most of all we want them to do *something*. Usually it is fair.

Zsuzsanna Budapest (Women's Spirituality Forum)
I charge for everything one hundred dollars.

Phaedra Bonewits (Ár nDraíocht Féin)
I haven't done so for a long time, but Isaac did weddings pretty regularly. What he did and what I recommend is charging what is the going rate for such services from other ministers or professional wedding officiants. Also, the time it takes to meet with the couple, write or compile the wedding, attend the rehearsal, and everything else (travel time!) has to be factored into the fee. It's far more than just the ceremony itself.

More like $300-$600, depending on what's required. Is it just show up and sign the license? Is it meet with the couple, write a custom ceremony, come the night before for a rehearsal, a lot of driving, and maybe an overnight stay? $100 does not cut it.

I just hate the way Pagan clergy undervalue their services. Call around and see what a UU minister would charge or look online for non-denominational ministers and see what they charge. A hundred bucks is nothing.

Rev. Laura Wildman-Hanlon (Wiccan High Priestess, professional wedding officiant)
For weddings/handfastings, I ask a sliding scale from $100 to $150, depending upon how much time I'm going to be involved and how much money the couple is spending for their wedding. I always emphasize I will not turn anyone away. If the couple is spending $10,000 on their wedding then they can afford to pay their Clergy. On the other hand, if they are just starting off and don't have more than $10 to their names, I'm not going to take it. In their case, a hug is more than sufficient. What I am charging for is my time and skills at designing rituals which will hopefully touch the hearts of all involved.

Ed Fitch (Pagan Way; Gardnerian High Priest)
I make no written or verbal requests for my services, as I consider Clergy duties as part of my life's calling. Even so, the people for whom I am providing these services invariably will quietly pay me $50 to $150 afterwards. Of course, if I did not already have my pensions from industry and my military years, and needed to pay my own living expenses, I might possibly pre-bill for my services.

Sam Webster (Pantheon Foundation)
Generally, if they are a member of your congregation, they are already paying for your services. Otherwise the going rate is $100.

Pyrokanthos (Aquarian Order of the Restoration; Thiasos Olympikos, Rhinoceros Lodge)
When people have asked me to perform weddings they often ask if there is a fee. I tell them that I don't charge for a sacrament, which marriage is, but that people often do make contributions, and that if they want to, they can. Often that is basically the

going rate, which can be anywhere from $50 to, in one case, over a thousand. If they want to know an amount, I tell them to give what they can afford; that usually turns out to be more than I would have asked. As it is also a legal thing, there is paperwork to fill out and mail, signatures to get, and all that. I have to herd them for that part, and make sure they have done all the legal stuff beforehand.

I usually do counseling beforehand and tell them to call me if they have problems afterward. They never do, until it is too late.

I have never charged anybody for a funeral. I have figured they had enough to deal with. I suppose some people might want to make a contribution, but frankly, I usually get people who have little background with Clergy and who are trying to get by.

If I have to travel, I do ask that expenses be paid, for sure. Gas, etc. If it is an overnighter, then I need a place to stay. Sometimes somebody puts me up in a room, sometimes they get me a motel room.

From "The 4th Wise Man" by Tom Foster, 1971.

Appendix 7:
Performing Marriages

From "Universal Life Church," *Wikipedia*

WITHIN THE UNITED STATES, ALL FIFTY STATES THEORETICALLY authorize ministers who are ordained and authorized by their church to officiate marriages. In most states, ordination as a minister is the only requirement for a minister to be able to officiate lawful weddings. Some states require additional documentation, such as a "letter of good standing" or that the minister present his or her credential of ordination and register. One state, Missouri, also requires that the minister must be a United States citizen, and some states specify that the minister must be at least 18 years of age (although this is probably a presumed requirement in all states, since the minister will attest to a legal document).

Some states do not even require actual ordination, but permit those who declare themselves to be ministers to officiate marriage. ULC ministers wishing to perform legal weddings should refer to the local authority in the jurisdiction where the marriage is to occur for specific information about jurisdictional issues and requirements.

Outside the U.S., some countries are very liberal in this regard. Japan, for example, will recognize anyone who claims him- or herself to be a minister, regardless of church affiliation. Many developing countries are also quite liberal in their restrictions and definitions.

On the other hand, several major countries are quite restrictive. In Canada, ULC ministers have been authorized to solemnize marriage only in a few local jurisdictions. In many other countries, ULC ministers have no authority to solemnize lawful marriage. Some ministers avoid this complication by meeting requirements to solemnize a civil ceremony, which might include being registered as a notary public or a justice of the peace. In some places, such as Saudi Arabia and Iran, religion and government are one, and anyone caught promoting a religious practice outside of the government complex can be subjected to severe punishment.

In many countries, including much of continental Europe, Turkey, Japan and the countries of the former Soviet Union, only marriages performed by the state in a civil ceremony are recognized legally. It is customary for couples who wish a religious— or any other—ceremony to hold one separately from the civil wedding.

Appendix 8:
Premarital Counseling

By Rhiannon Zell

WHY PREMARITAL COUNSELING? OFTEN A COUPLE WILL APPROACH a Priest or Priestess asking them to do a handfasting or legal marriage. It is important, if it is a legal marriage, to discover where the couple are planning to marry and to check what the requirements are in that state (see Appendix 1). Some states require prior registration in the state, fees, etc. Other than the legal issue, from here on, we will use the term "marriage" for both handfastings and legal marriages. Many couples do not expect premarital counseling, but it is highly recommended. Research has found it reduces the risk of separation or divorce by up to 30%. In addition to aiding in providing a wedding experience that each partner finds meaningful, it can help a couple build a stronger relationship and see obstacles that may arise in the future, and make plans and find strategies that help overcome them.

Premarital counseling will take several sessions; I usually try to plan for four, including the planning of the ceremony.

Myths

Many people enter into relationships with the thought that the relationship will take away their problems and make life perfect. Deep in debt, they believe the partnership will overcome their money issues, or feeling lonely, they feel their partner will make everything bad disappear. The truth is, marriage is a relationship of "mutual interdependency". It depends on what each person puts into it, but it becomes more than those parts. It is love, and caring, and hard work. It is not a magical "cure-all". However, when people enter it with problems, those problems intensify unless both partners are aware and willing to work on solving them. Premarital counseling is designed to help people become aware of both the positives and negatives, and recognize how they each tend to meet those issues.

There are four characteristics that tend to make an enduring relationship. They are:
1. Faithfulness/Honesty
2. Work Ethic/Financial Responsibility
3. Spiritual Compatibility
4. Sense of Humor

Counseling

The easiest way to approach premarital counseling is looking at various issues, and asking guiding questions for each individual to answer and discuss.

Start out with just a simple "getting to know you". Questions like "How did you meet?", "How has the relationship been so far?", and "Tell me what you like most about your partner." This gives you an opportunity to get to know the couple, and learn some of their strengths and get a feel for the relationship.

Other areas to explore include:

Attitude/beliefs toward marriage – What is marriage? Why do you want to get married? What do you think will change? Have you been married before? If so, what is your relationship now? Any children from past relationships? How much time/attention do you expect from your spouse?

Money – Explore each person's ideas about spending and saving (including long-term things like retirement, and shorter-term investments like appliances, car, house). What is your current financial situation? Are you in debt? What plans do you have for getting out of debt? Who will be responsible for handling the financial issues? For investment decisions? Have you taken (or do you need) a money-management course for couples?(many places United Way offers free or low-cost courses such as this).

Emotions and Conflict – Has each person learned how to tell the other what they expect (instead of the other having to be a mind-reader)? Have they learned how to listen and discuss? How have they managed conflict so far? Is this working or does it need to change? Is there anything they are NOT prepared to give up in this marriage? How do they react when they are angry? How will they resolve differences? What skills do they need to acquire in this area?

Sex – Is this a closed or open marriage? What are their ideas on monogamy> What are the boundaries? Are their any problems with sexual health (sexually transmitted diseases, herpes, Hepatitis C, etc)? Does their body image affect their sexuality? Can they be honest about this with their partner? Are there past experiences that may affect the sexual relationship (sexual abuse, rape, abuse in general, fears, etc)? Can they be open with the partner about these experiences? Are there certain sexual preferences (such as preferred times, place, lighting, length of activity, foreplay; how adventurous is a partner willing to be?)

Affection – upon leaving each day, what is expected (a wave goodbye, a kiss, an embrace? How do they each feel about public displays of affection? Display in front of their children if they are to have any? What is expected at anniversaries (and what anniversaries are celebrated?), birthdays, holidays? What of gift exchanges, flowers, etc?

Children – Do they want children? How many? When? How wil they affect the careen, lifestyle, recreation, privacy, social interests, money, and future plans? What of unexpected pregnancies, possible infertilifity, miscarriages, birth defects, etc?

Equality – what name will the couple go by? Will neither, either, or both change their name or hyphenate names? If there are children, what last name will they take?

Work – Will both work? Does one or both want to finish training or education? Can they afford the change in income if it changes? How does each deal with job stress? With shift work? Will each be expected to be available by cell phone or other at any time? What of work that has to be taken home because of job expectations?

Household – Does each have the same expectations and standards in housekeeping (for instance: how clean is the house expected to be? What time are meals- do you eat together and where do you eat? How much time is spent watching TV or playing games on the computer?) What is the division of labor (who will wash dishes, vacuum, mow lawn, do outside chores, etc) – especially if children are involved?

Pet Peeves – What things bother you the most, and how much "personal space" and "alone time" does each need?

Friends – Do you like and respect each other's friends? Are they welcome anytime, or just when invited? Who else may have access to the house key? What if there are no friends? What are the boundaries and limits? What of friends of the opposite sex?

Family – Looking at each other's families give a good insight into the other person. How involved will the families be? Are they welcome anytime or just when invited? How much involvement do they have in decisions?

Religion – Do you share the same beliefs? If not, how accepting are they of the other's beliefs? How will children be raised? Are the families of the same beliefs, and if not, how accepting are they? Are there individual practices that need to be accommodated?

The Ceremony

If you have been asked to perform the wedding or handfasting, remember to check if they want a legal ceremony first, and check Appendix 1 for requirements. Frequently the couple (or at least the bride) will have definite ideas on what they want. They should be responsible for most of the arrangements, but may need guidance. Some things to consider are:

1. Where will the ceremony be held?
2. Who and how many will be attending (is it Pagan only, or a mix, or Christian, etc?)
3. How formal, and what should the one officiating wear?
4. Do they want to write their own ceremony, vows, etc, or shall you, or is their one that they have found that they wish to use? (go over the ceremony with them before to be certain it fits their needs).
5. Will others be involved in the ceremony?
6. Will there be music they wish to include?
7. Will there be a rehearsal (especially if formal) that you are expected to conduct, or any other tasks you will be expected to take care of?
8. If a handfasting, will it be for "a year and a day" as traditional first-handfastings were, or for longer (we recommend NOT doing them "for eternity" or "forever"— breaking such a binding, if it turns out to have too many problems, is very difficult).
9. Discuss alternative plans for weather if the ceremony is going to be held outdoors.

In Summary

Premarital counseling is not required but is highly recommended. You are acting as a guide for the couple to explore their relationship and need to refrain from making decisions for them or judging the decisions they make for themselves. Be aware of what your own answers to some of these questions would be and recognize that although those answers are right for you, they may not be right for all. It is considered proper to recommend budgeting classes if they seem clueless on money management, or anger management training if that is an issue, etc. If there is an area you feel totally uncomfortable with, you can recommend some questions that they discuss amongst themselves. If you see issues arise where you feel out of your depth, feel free to refer to a professional. Try to have a list of resources on hand.

Appendix 9:
Marriage Laws
of Various States

Provided by the International Clergy Association, Monterey, California
[NOTE: CAW sanctions and performs both same-sex and poly marriages.]

PERFORMING MARRIAGES IS BOTH ENJOYABLE AND SATISFYING. You need have no hesitation as long as you follow the laws and procedures in your state. Our purpose is to let you know, in general, the laws of your state and to let you know where to go to get the necessary forms and information. Most states do not require a particular kind of ceremony. They leave that to the church in question. Those states that have requirements regarding the ceremony simply state that the bride and groom must say to each other, in the presence of the minister and the witnesses, that they take each other as husband and wife. The rest of the ceremony may be a traditional one or may be made up by the couple and/or the minister.

Before you perform a marriage ceremony, you must be sure that the couple has a valid marriage license. Look at the license and any other papers that come with it to see what is required of you. Usually all you have to do is complete the blank spaces on the marriage license itself. There should be a space for the couple, the minister, and the witnesses to sign. Also, you may be required to provide the couple with a marriage certificate. When marriage certificates are required, they are usually provided with the marriage license. You will probably be required to return the license and other papers to the county clerk or other official within a certain number of days.

California has a special law which allows an unmarried man and woman who have been "living together as man and wife" to marry without a license or a blood test. If you want to perform this type of marriage, you should tell the couple to go to the county clerk's office and obtain form VS-123 which is called "Authorization and Certificate of Confidential Marriage." There is a charge for the form of between $25 and $30. Only persons who are at least 18 years old may be married in this manner. The names of the couple married this way are not published in the "Vital Statistics" section of the newspaper and copies of form VS-123 are only available to the couple being married. Other people must have a court order to see the form or to obtain a copy. (Of course, the couple may provide copies of the form to anyone they wish.) The idea behind this is to provide a way for people who have been living together to be married without the embarrassment of admitting in public that they were not really married in the first place. This law was made in the 1800's! We do not know of similar laws in other states.

In most states you are allowed to advertise that you will perform marriages and you may usually charge any fee you feel is appropriate. However, some states such as Kentucky forbid ministers to solicit marriages.

The laws of all states allow ministers to perform marriages. Nevertheless, we have compiled a summary of state marriage laws to let you know what you must do to perform marriages in your state. Under each state we quote or paraphrase what the law has to say about ministers who may perform marriages.

You will find that many states say that "ordained or licensed ministers" may perform marriages. Here "licensed" means licensed by the church. In addition to being ordained and licensed by the church. some states require the minister to be registered with the state or city before performing marriages. If such a state or city requirement exists in your state, we will say so in the summary. If there is no mention of registration, probably none is required by your state. In the summary of state laws. we also let you know what record keeping must be done after you perform a marriage and we will tell you what official to see if you have other questions about performing marriages.

We have spent many hours in the law library developing this information and we have made every effort to be sure that what we have said is accurate. However, we cannot be certain that we have not overlooked something. Also, laws change from time to time and there could be changes of which we are not aware. Therefore, you should verify this information with your county clerk. You might even want to go to a local law library or even a regular public library and look up the law for yourself.

From time to time a few places have made it difficult or impossible for "mail-order" ministers to perform marriages. Our own feeling is that this is an unconstitutional practice, but it would be expensive to institute a lawsuit to correct the matter. Since a United States Circuit Court Judge has ruled in favor of "mail-order" ministers, it should be clear to all that you are legally entitled to perform marriages.

If you should have any difficulty, we would be interested in hearing about it.
www.usit.com/tnglmoon/marriage-laws.htm

Marriage Laws by State - WeddingWire
www.weddingwire.com/wedding-ideas/marriage-laws-by-state

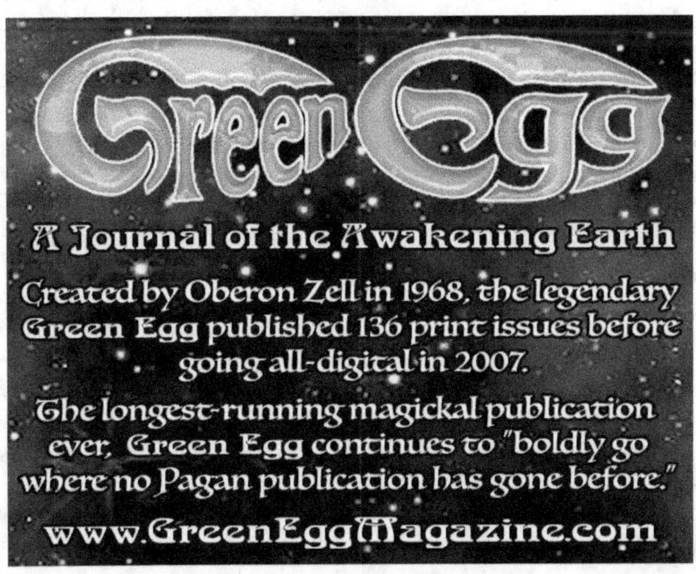

Appendix 10:
The Advanced Bonewits' Cult Danger Evaluation Frame 2.7

by Isaac Bonewits (© 1979, 2008 c.e.)

Introduction

Events in the last several decades have clearly indicated just how dangerous some religious and secular groups (usually called "cults" by those opposed to them) can be to their own members as well as to anyone else whom they can influence. "Brainwashing," beatings, child abuse, rapes, murders, mass suicides, military drilling and gunrunning, meddling in civil governments, international terrorism, and other crimes have been charged against leaders and members of many groups, and in far too many cases those accusations have been correct. None of this has been very surprising to historians of religion or to other scholars of what are usually labeled "new" religions (no matter how old they may be in their cultures of origin). Minority groups, especially religious ones, are often accused of crimes by members of the current majority. In many ways, for example, the "Mormons" were the "Moonies" of the 19th century — at least in terms of being an unusual minority belief system that many found "shocking" at the time — and the members of the Unification Church could be just as "respectable" a hundred years from now as the Latter Day Saints are today.

Nonetheless, despite all the historical and philosophical warnings that could be issued, ordinary people faced with friends or loved ones joining an "unusual" group, or perhaps contemplating joining one themselves, need a relatively simple way to evaluate just how dangerous or harmless a given group is liable to be, without either subjecting themselves to its power or judging it solely on theological or ideological grounds (the usual method used by anti-cult groups).

In 1979 I constructed an evaluation tool which I now call the "Advanced Bonewits' Cult Danger Evaluation Frame" or the "ABCDEF" (because evaluating these groups should be elementary). A copy was included in that year's revised edition of my book, Real Magic. I realize its shortcomings, but feel that it can be effectively used to separate harmless groups from the potentially dangerous ones and distinguish harmful ones from those that are merely unusual to the observer. Feedback from those attempting to use the system has always been appreciated. Indirect feedback, in terms of the number of places on and off the Net this ABCDEF has shown up, has been mostly favorable. It has been used by the Federal Bureau of Investigation in its Meddigo Report on Bible-based cults (which really bothered some members of the Religious Reich). It was also used by the government of the Union of South Africa, in its report on minority religions. This latter led to the legalization of same-sex marriage there. It has appeared in a few books by other Pagan authors as part of discussions about choosing ethical teachers and groups.

The purpose of this evaluation tool is to help both amateur and professional observers, including current or would-be members, of various organizations (including religious, occult, psychological or political groups) to determine just how dangerous a given group is liable to be, in comparison with other groups, to the physical and mental health of its members and of other people subject to its influence. It cannot speak to the "spiritual dangers," if any, that might be involved, for the simple reason that one person's path to enlightenment or "salvation" is often viewed by another as a path to ignorance or "damnation."

As a general rule, the higher the numerical total scored by a given group (the further to the right of the scale), the more dangerous it is likely to be. Though it is obvious that many of the scales in the frame are subjective, it is still possible to make practical judgments using it, at least of the "is this group more dangerous than that one?" sort. This is **if** all numerical assignments are based on accurate and unbiased observation of **actual behavior** by the groups and their top levels of leadership (as distinct from official pronouncements). This means that you need to pay attention to what the secondary and tertiary leaders are saying and doing, as much (or more so) than the central leadership — after all, "plausible deniability" is not a recent historical invention.

This tool can be used by parents, reporters, law enforcement agents, social scientists and others interested in evaluating the actual dangers presented by a given group or movement. Obviously, different observers will achieve differing degrees of precision, depending upon the sophistication of their numerical assignments on each scale. However, if the same observers use the same methods of scoring and weighting each scale, their comparisons of relative danger or harmlessness between groups will be reasonably valid, at least for their own purposes. People who cannot, on the other hand, view competing belief systems as ever having possible spiritual value to anyone, will find the ABCDEF annoyingly useless for promoting their theological agendas. Worse, these members of the Religious Reich and their fellow theocrats will find that their own organizations (and quite a few large mainstream churches) are far more "cult-like" than many of the minority belief systems they so bitterly oppose.

It should be pointed out that the ABCDEF is founded upon both modern psychological theories about mental health and personal growth, and my many years of participant observation and historical research into minority belief systems. Those who believe that relativism and anarchy are as dangerous to mental health as absolutism and authoritarianism, could (I suppose) count groups with total scores nearing either extreme (high or low) as being equally hazardous. As far as dangers to physical well-being are concerned, however, both historical records and current events clearly indicate the direction in which the greatest threats lie. This is especially so since the low-scoring groups usually seem to have survival and growth rates so small that they seldom develop the abilities to commit large scale atrocities even had they the philosophical or political inclinations to do so.

Advanced Bonewits' Cult Danger Evaluation Frame
(version 2.6)

	Factors:		1 2 3 4 5 6 7 8 9 10 Low High
1	**Internal Control:** Amount of internal political and social power exercised by leader(s) over members; lack of clearly defined organizational rights for members.	1	____________________
2	**External Control:** Amount of external political and social influence desired or obtained; emphasis on directing members' external political and social behavior.	2	____________________
3	**Wisdom/Knowledge Claimed** by leader(s); amount of infallibility declared or implied about decisions or doctrinal/scriptural interpretations; number and degree of unverified and/or unverifiable credentials claimed.	3	____________________
4	**Wisdom/Knowledge Credited** to leader(s) by members; amount of trust in decisions or doctrinal/scrip-tural interpretations made by leader(s); amount of hostility by members towards internal or external critics and/or towards verification efforts.	4	____________________
5	**Dogma:** Rigidity of reality concepts taught; amount of doctrinal inflexibil-ity or "fundamentalism;" hostility towards relativism and situationalism.	5	____________________
6	**Recruiting:** Emphasis put on attracting new members; amount of proselytizing; requirement for all members to bring in new ones.	6	____________________

#		#	
7	**Front Groups:** Number of subsidiary groups using different names from that of main group, especially when connections are hidden.	7	____________________
8	**Wealth:** Amount of money and/or property desired or obtained by group; emphasis on members' donations; economic lifestyle of leader(s) compared to ordinary members.	8	____________________
9	**Sexual Manipulation** of members by leader(s) of non-tantric groups; amount of control exercised over sexuality of members in terms of sexual orientation, behavior, and/or choice of partners.	9	____________________
10	**Sexual Favoritism:** Advancement or preferential treatment dependent upon sexual activity with the leader(s) of non-tantric groups.	10	____________________
11	**Censorship:** Amount of control over members' access to outside opinions on group, its doctrines or leader(s).	11	____________________
12	**Isolation:** Amount of effort to keep members from communicating with non-members, including family, friends and lovers.	12	____________________
13	**Dropout Control:** Intensity of efforts directed at preventing or returning dropouts.	13	____________________
14	**Violence:** Amount of approval when used by or for the group, its doctrines or leader(s).	14	____________________
15	**Paranoia:** Amount of fear concerning real or imagined enemies; exaggeration of perceived power of opponents; prevalence of conspiracy theories.	15	____________________
16	**Grimness:** Amount of disapproval concerning jokes about the group, its doctrines or its leader(s).	16	____________________

17	**Surrender of Will:** Amount of emphasis on members not having to be responsible for personal decisions; degree of individual disempowerment created by the group, its doctrines or its leader(s).	**17**	
18	**Hypocrisy:** amount of approval for actions which the group officially considers immoral or unethical, when done by or for the group, its doctrines or leader(s); willingness to violate the group's declared principles for political, psychological, social, economic, military, or other gain.	**18**	
			1 2 3 4 5 6 7 8 9 10 **Low** **High**

A Dutch translation of this is available at *Bonewits' Geavanceerde Raamwerk ter Evaluatie van Sektegevaar*

A German translation of the 2.0 version of this is available at: *Isaac Bonewits' Sektengefahr Checkliste*.

A French translation of the 2.6 version is available at: *Grille avancée de Bonewits pour l'évaluation du danger potentiel d'une secte*.

An Italian translation of the 2.6 version is available at: *Documento Avanzato di Isaac Bonewits per la Valutazione del Pericolo del Culto*.

A Polish translation of the 2.6 version is available at: *Zaawansowany Kwestionariusz Bonewitsa Oceniajacy Niebezpieczenstwo Sekty*

A Portuguese translation of the 2.6 version is available at: *A Ferramenta Avançada de Bonewits para Avaliação de Seitas.*

Other translations will be posted as they are done.